HAUNTED WORLD

To Ruthie and Matthew, Robbie and Kaitlyn:
May this book be a light for you
in dark places when all
other lights go out.

'There are more things in heaven and earth, Horatio,
Than are dreamt of in your philosophy.'

Hamlet,
Shakespeare

HAUNTED WORLD

101 Ghostly Places and Encounters

THERESA CHEUNG

Michael O'Mara Books Limited

First published in Great Britain in 2024 by
Michael O'Mara Books Limited
9 Lion Yard
Tremadoc Road
London SW4 7NQ

A CIP catalogue record for this book is available from the British Library.

This product is made of material from well-managed, FSC®-certified forests and other controlled sources. The manufacturing processes conform to the environmental regulations of the country of origin.

ISBN: 978-1-78929-580-1 in paperback print format
ISBN: 978-1-78929-713-3 in hardback print format
ISBN: 978-1-78929-581-8 in ebook format

1 2 3 4 5 6 7 8 9 10

Cover design by Ana Bjezancevic
Designed and typeset by Claire Cater
Illustrations by Alessandro Valdrighi
Printed and bound by CPI Group (UK) Ltd, Croydon, CR0 4YY

MIX
Paper | Supporting
responsible forestry
FSC® C171272
www.fsc.org

CONTENTS

FOREWORD BY LOYD AUERBACH

Here's a true statement: our world is haunted!

It's haunted by our history, memories, folklore and legends, all of which contribute to the idea of places, objects and people being *haunted* in the more psychic or paranormal sense. Interest and belief in ghostly things has been with us for thousands of years and clearly is still with us today. That interest led to the start of the field of psychical research in the 1880s (later called parapsychology), along with the development of more mainstream empirical sciences around the same time.

As a parapsychologist who has specialized in investigating and researching cases and experiences of apparitions, hauntings and poltergeists for over forty years, it's been clear that our fascination with people, places and things called 'paranormal' or 'psychic' has not waned in the technological age but has actually increased in visibility and popularity thanks to popular culture and social media.

Ghost-hunting-focused reality television shows continue to multiply, and due to the number of these shows, so does the number of hobbyist and amateur ghost-hunting/paranormal investigating groups. One issue that crops up for both the viewers and the producers of these shows has to do with location. As the shows take on-screen talent to haunted places, the producers are constantly on the lookout for 'new' haunted places to keep up the interest of their viewers. In addition, the shows often present slightly (sometimes greatly) altered backstories for those locations, as well as being edited to make the investigations more dramatic and viewer-friendly. This has led to new folklore about so many places, whether they are actually 'active' (meaning there have been recent reports of hauntings) or not. In fact, when one digs into the actual history and reported paranormal occurrences of many of the haunted locations featured on television, a very different story often emerges. Fascinatingly, though, the truth is sometimes even stranger and more interesting than what producers choose to showcase.

This increasing interest in all things ghostly has led to the development of a kind of 'paranormal tourism', with many haunted locations offering ghost tours and special events, whether directed at serious ghost-hunting groups or simply the paranormally curious. On the plus side, many historical locations have been able to access increased financial support, even fixing the places up, due to so many paranormal tourists. On the downside, some locations featured on TV have found themselves at the centre of too much attention (and even demands) from ghost-hunting groups, finding that their historical sites have become synonymous with eerie ghost sightings.

The book you're about to read takes a good look at many known and legendary haunted locations. The real-life histories of these locations are often more captivating – and oftentimes more horrifying – than the witness reports of disembodied knockings and ethereal voices, but it is also these latter stories that make it or break it for those who want to visit the sites and be entertained (which we all want to experience when hearing or reading a ghost story). Parapsychologists use slightly different terms and conceptualizations of the phenomena and stay away from using terms commonly used in popular culture, like 'demon' and even 'supernatural'. We even have good explanations for things like orbs in photos and videos, following over 140 years of investigations and research in this field.

But when it comes to visiting a haunted house or other location, the story *is* the thing. We want to be enthralled, thrilled and perhaps even a little creeped out. The locations and the entries accompanying them in this fascinating book by Theresa Cheung will lead you to great spots and most definitely leave a chill up your spine!

Loyd Auerbach

Director, Office of Paranormal Investigation
President, Forever Family Foundation
President, Rhine Research Center Board of Directors
Adjunct Professor, Atlantic University

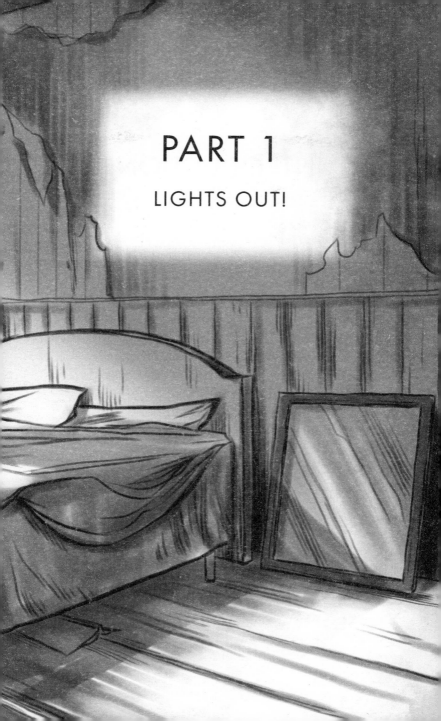

PART 1

LIGHTS OUT!

INTRODUCTION

'A house is never still in darkness to those who
listen intently; there is a whispering in distant
chambers, an unearthly hand presses the snib
of the window, the latch rises. Ghosts were
created when the first person woke in the night.'

The Little Minister,
J. M. Barrie

It started with a mirror.

Decades ago, when I first moved to London – rich in youth and a sense of adventure but poor in cash and a sense of direction – I worked for a while as a 'serving wench' in the Beefeater by the Tower of London. In its day, this historical re-enactment, complete with flickering torchlight, Henry VIII tribute artist, strolling players, jousting knights and all-singing, all-dancing serving wenches, was a quintessentially British, boisterous recreation of a Tudor banquet – or how everyone imagines it to be. Tourists from all over the world eagerly devoured it.

One night, as I was quietly reading a book and enjoying the calm of a few minutes' break in the staff changing room, I heard a rustling sound behind me. I looked up. In the dressing table mirror in front of me, I glimpsed a pale-looking woman in a floaty, long-sleeved white dress, swaying from side to side a few feet behind me. I turned around, but there was no one there.

I don't remember feeling alarmed. I was working in a Tudor recreation after all, so I assumed it was probably another staff member in costume who had swiftly exited the changing room. I returned to my book. I heard the rustling again. This time when I looked up in the mirror, the pale lady wasn't a few feet away but standing right behind me. I noticed her sparkling blue tiara, which matched her blue eyes. Again, when I turned around to say hello, nobody was there.

In the moment, I put it down to the power of suggestion given the environment I was working in (not to mention the book I was reading, a collection of Edgar Allan Poe stories), but I couldn't escape the feeling that this vision felt very real. The most surprising thing was that the pale lady didn't scare me in the slightest. I sensed that whoever or whatever she was, and for whatever reason she was revealing herself to me, she meant me no harm.

In the evenings that followed, I found myself returning to sit in front of the mirror in the hope of seeing her again, but I never did. When I shared my story with a few of the other cast members, most rolled their eyes and suggested I was dreaming or had been drinking. I have always had vivid dreams, but I wasn't asleep when I saw her and I don't drink. A few colleagues mentioned that the Tower of London allegedly had many ghosts, so perhaps she was straying from there. It wasn't until my last day of working at the Beefeater that one of the strolling players took me aside and told me I wasn't the only one – she had seen the pale lady in the mirror too.

Was this woman I glimpsed in the mirror my first sighting of an actual ghost? Or was I simply imagining her? I don't know, but one thing is certain: it whetted my appetite and I began to properly research the supernatural from that time onwards. And all these years later, whenever I glimpse my reflection in a mirror, I know a part of me is still searching for her.

I have had other unexplained visions since then, mostly of dancing shadows and flickers in the corner of my eye. None of them have been quite so visceral – or seen with my wide-awake eyes – as the pale lady in the mirror. Often it happens just as I'm about to fall asleep, so I'm never sure if I am dreaming or awake. Typically, the experience is subtle and could easily be a trick of the light. But each time the experience feels very real. It is also unforgettable – it quite literally haunts me – and if I close my eyes and take myself back to the vision, I can relive it in intense detail.

These supernatural experiences didn't stop with my glimpse of I'm-not-sure-what in a mirror. On one occasion, I believe a disembodied voice may have saved my life. If the pale lady was a catalyst to ignite my desire to see the other side more clearly, this experience encouraged me to have a little more faith in my own potential mediumistic abilities.

I was in my early thirties. I found myself driving behind a slow-moving van that was impossible to overtake due to oncoming traffic. We reached a junction. I needed to turn left, as that was the fastest route to my destination, ensuring I would arrive on time for my first ever radio interview. I was excited for this new opportunity, which was why hearing the voice of my departed mother telling me to 'take the right path' while I was waiting at the junction was wildly unexpected. The voice – which I had already heard in my dreams the night before – seemed to be coming from both inside and outside my head at the same time, and it was so calm, clear and decisive, I did not hesitate to obey. I instinctively turned right and missed my radio slot because the roundabout route to my destination from that point involved heavy traffic delays. I cursed silently to myself all the way home.

Frustration transformed into shock when I found out later that evening that if I had turned left as intended, chances are I *might* have been involved in a fatal crash. A pile-up close to the junction that happened moments after I had turned in the other direction tragically killed three people. The van I had been trailing was involved in the crash.

Was this really the voice of my mother in spirit warning me, or was it simply a memory, as she always used to tell me to take the right path in life, meaning do the right thing? Or was it my impatience about being stuck behind a van that made me irrationally turn right? I will never know for sure, of course, but it's something I often reflect deeply about.

I'm very aware that seeing things that aren't there and hearing voices is often said to be one of the first signs of madness. Although my family may at times disagree, I'm most certainly not mad. I don't suffer from hallucinations or anxiety. I have gone through every possible explanation, and I feel sure that both the woman in the mirror and the mysterious voice while I was driving were not things I imagined. These unexplained, spontaneous experiences, whatever they were, *happened* to me. All these decades later, I am no longer ashamed to admit to them.

And I know from the countless afterlife stories I receive from my readers and listeners that their uncanny experiences happened to them too. Many of them begin their stories by saying that they really aren't sure if life after death exists or if ghosts are real or if this was all in their imagination, but this is their story. It felt real, it still feels real, and they can't explain or forget it. Many are relieved to share their stories, sometimes for the first time, and to be taken seriously.

For the past thirty years I have written an endless stream of supernatural books and psychic world encyclopaedias, and in recent years have become a go-to TV, radio and podcast expert on matters paranormal. My career has been dedicated to researching, writing about and talking about ghosts, hauntings, dreams and the psychic world. I'm on a mission to mainstream the supernatural. But it's not just been the theme of my career, it's been the direction and the passion of my entire life.

I was born into a family of psychics and spiritualists, where talk of 'seeing dead people' was commonplace. My earliest memory of attending a seance or mediumship demonstration was around the age of five or six. At the time, I had no idea what was going on. I didn't see any spooks or tables turning, but I did see a lot of crying and a lot of smiling and often the two happening together.

Growing up, I was plagued with self-doubt and square peg/round hole syndrome as a result of my inability to *consciously* connect to the other side as a medium or psychic allegedly can – but despite this, I have always had a strong belief in the afterlife. This was not just because of my spiritualist upbringing but because of my academic study of the metaphysical world while doing my degree in Theology and English at King's College, Cambridge. What followed was a lifetime of research into the possibility of ghosts, which has shaped my writing career. I've been lucky enough to collaborate with academics, doctors, neuroscientists, psychiatrists, psychologists and parapsychologists researching the science of consciousness, as well as authentic mediums and psychics. And, most important of all, I've had hundreds of discussions with people who believe they have been through paranormal experiences.

Along the way, my conviction has been constantly boosted by the deluge of messages I gratefully continue to receive from people all over the world sharing their true-life ghostly experiences. These people come from all backgrounds and stages of life. I believe that every experience of a ghost or haunting should be treated with the utmost respect. They are an undying part of the human experience, and instead of dismissing or denying them, I believe that we need to strive constantly to understand them better.

The idea of this book, apart from sharing fascinating and compelling ghost stories, is to help you better understand the age-old and globally reported phenomena of ghosts and hauntings. I also hope it will circumvent some of the jargon that many ghost hunters and paranormal researchers easily lose themselves in, making what is a commonly reported human experience feel unnecessarily complicated, impenetrable, elite and specialist. I believe that once we lose our fear of the idea of an afterlife and of being left alone in the dark, we all have the potential to 'see' beyond the material world. Spirits can communicate in countless invisible ways that are unique to each of us. Yes, there are dramatic ghost sightings out there – and this book will showcase some very famous ones – but in general, full-blown apparitions are exceedingly rare and indeed no more or less helpful to our understanding of the afterlife than the quieter ones.

And just as you don't need to 'see' ghosts to believe in them, you really don't necessarily need to seek out the services of ghost hunters or mediums either. This book will show that you can become your own psychical researcher, your own medium. All you need is curiosity, a willingness to go outside your comfort zone and a hefty dose of self-belief and common sense. And if you have had (or after reading this book, go on to have) a paranormal experience, I want you to feel reassured that it is *not* something to panic about or deny. It is something to get excited about and to discuss with people who are non-judgemental. Every report of a haunting is a reminder that there is so much more to this life – and to being a human, to being amazing you – than meets the eye.

AFTERLIFE

Ghost stories typically peak in popularity when times are uncertain because people are more inclined to seek answers, a sense of connection and some deeper meaning to life in unconventional ways when they are not finding answers in the usual places. We saw this after both world wars, for example, when there was a boom in spiritualism connected to the human need to process grief, and more recently reports of hauntings spiked during the COVID pandemic. But whatever is happening in the world, there will always be an enduring fascination with ghosts simply because they encourage us to tackle head-on the biggest question and mystery of all: what happens when we die?

Before touching on what science currently suggests about the possibility of an afterlife, it is important to get some clarity on commonly used terminology.

Spirit

The spirit refers to the invisible consciousness, soul or essence of a person that can exist independently of their body (discarnate/disembodied) and which is believed to survive bodily death. Spirits can also personify places and forces of nature, such as lakes, forests, mountains and the elements. The term is often used to describe all non-physical entities, including ghosts. In general, spirits are said to have found their peace in the afterlife, whereas ghosts have not.

Ghost

This is a popular term for the spirit of a departed person that is visible to or experienced in some way by the living. Ghosts tend to be solitary and linger in the places they lived when they were alive. They can resemble the human form but are also often witnessed as translucent and therefore described as fog-like, misty or transparent. Their presence can also be sensed or felt as cold air, strange noises, energy shifts and unexplained smells.

It is believed that ghosts linger on earth because they have unfinished business and can't find peace. They may re-enact their death or scenes of trauma and intense emotion. Frederic Myers, one of the founders of the Society for Psychical Research (the SPR was set up in London in 1882 as the first scientific organization to examine claims of the paranormal; its American counterpart is the ASPR), believed ghosts were, to paraphrase, manifestations of persistent personal memory, or an indication that some kind of force is being exercised after death which is in some way connected to a person previously known on earth. Myers proposed that ghosts were projections of consciousness or memories from the past which have imprinted themselves on a location, but other paranormal experts believe that ghosts may have some form of awareness.

'Uncanny', 'spooky' and 'eerie' are all words that suggest a ghost or a haunting may be occurring, but they can simply mean something is mysterious or unexplained, or that something familiar is occurring in an unsettling or bizarre setting. Other commonly used terms for 'ghost' but with additional associations include:

Doppelgänger – ghostly double of someone who is living.
Phantom/phantasm – figment of the imagination.
Spectre – haunting that is typically proved to be explainable or fraudulent.
Spook – ghost that can assume human form.
Wraith – spirit of a living person on the brink of death.

Apparition

This is the inexplicable appearance of a person, animal, entity or object that can't be explained rationally. Most apparitions are of objects in the physical world or of a living person, but apparitions of the dead are also called ghosts. Psychical researchers prefer to use the term apparition.

Haunting

It is a common misconception that a haunting involves a sighting of a ghost, spirit or apparition. This can be the case, but the great majority of hauntings involve anomalous cold spots, noises, smells and physical sensations. There may also be unexplained movement of objects, doors and windows opening inexplicably, and electrical appliances behaving erratically. People visiting haunted locations may also experience intense, unexplained emotions.

The term 'haunt' comes from the same word root as home, so it implies an occupation of a home or place by the spirits of dead people or animals who once lived there. However, some hauntings occur at places the deceased person never visited or where trauma or death occurred. In some cases there may be no association with the place at all or even motivation for the haunting. Some hauntings are reported for centuries, others only for a brief time, while others are reported only once or occur at similar times each year. Not every person who visits an allegedly haunted site will experience paranormal phenomena. It is said that only those who are emotionally or psychically receptive at the time can pick up the sensations.

Supernatural

This term refers to transcendental (spiritual) phenomena and inhuman entities that may exist outside the laws of science and nature or in alternative realities, such as ghosts, angels, demons and deities.

Occult

This is the term for supernatural ideas that fall outside of both science and religion.

Paranormal

This is the word used to describe phenomena that, until they are better understood and explained, appear to contradict current or traditional scientific knowledge, such as precognition (glimpsing the future) and so on.

Medium

A medium is a living person who claims to be able to communicate with the spirits of the departed, offering 'proof' of survival. This can happen one on one or in a seance, involving a group of people united in their desire to contact the dead. Many mediums are also psychics, people who claim to have paranormal abilities such as telepathy, clairvoyance etc.

Parapsychology

This field is the academic study of phenomena excluded from or inexplicable according to orthodox scientific psychology. A parapsychologist or psychical researcher investigates anomalous phenomena, sometimes in a lab setting.

Although I will continue to use the familiar terms 'paranormal' and 'supernatural' in this book, I am not a fan of either, as they suggest something additional, extra. I much prefer the term 'sixth sense' for feeling what is unseen and the term 'supernormal' for both paranormal and supernatural experiences, because sensing what is unseen and having mysterious experiences are part of being human – the norm, not the exception.

DO GHOSTS EXIST?

Even though definitive scientific proof isn't yet out there, many people believe ghosts are real. Surveys consistently show that at least one in four people believe they have encountered a ghost, and one in three people believe ghosts exist. Without a shadow of a doubt, belief in, as well as alleged experience of, ghosts and hauntings is most certainly out there. Film director Steven Spielberg was spot on when he said, 'Probably every fourth person you talk to has had an experience with a ghost or a poltergeist – or knows someone who has.'

Most hauntings have a logical explanation, but that leaves a tiny percentage that can't be explained. Here, briefly, are the main theories put forward by scientists and parapsychologists that attempt to explain the unexplainable.

Dream states

This refers to the hypnagogic state between waking and sleeping, and sleeping and waking. Dreams can sometimes feel incredibly real, and just before sleeping and immediately on waking, dream recall can be particularly vivid and mistaken for a paranormal experience. Sleep paralysis is also a perfectly natural state, when the body is asleep and unable to move but the brain remains conscious. Most of us don't recall sleep paralysis happening – we just fall asleep – but if you become aware of it happening, it can feel as if you are seeing real things with your eyes wide shut.

I'm one of the world's leading dream decoders, so this theory is one I have researched deeply. I've come to the conclusion that it can explain many cases but not all of them. I also believe the dream state has a lot to teach us about what is or is not real in our waking lives, as well as the possibility of an afterlife. Meeting departed loved ones in dreams, for example, has been shown to be therapeutic for those who are grieving. A hallmark of an afterlife dream is that it is vivid and realistic, and rather than being a series of random symbolic fragments, it has a beginning, a middle and an end.

Finding meaning in what is random

Terms for this, such as matrixing, pareidolia, and bottom-up and top-down processing, have subtle distinctions, but in essence all suggest ascribing meaning or images to what is random – for example, seeing angel shapes in the clouds or a divine image in a slice of buttered toast.

Inattentional or perceptual blindness are other related terms, where you only notice what you focus your attention on, missing the rest or what is obvious or contradictory. Anthropomorphizing, meanwhile, is attributing human characteristics to what is non-human.

Modern science is rapidly moving away from the belief that much of the natural world is random, and moving towards detecting some order in the chaos. We only need to look at the intricacies of a spider's web or the perfect symmetry of a snowflake or the unlimited efficiency of the human brain to understand the mathematical order of the universe. Quantum physics (the study of matter and energy within atoms) has revolutionized traditional scientific thinking by challenging the fundamental principle of cause preceding effect and assigning as much importance to the observer as to the observed.

I am not a scientist, but it does give us reason to suppose that life is more than just a complex arrangement of physical matter brought about by chance, opening up the infinite possibility of an interconnectedness or wholeness of the universe reminiscent of the belief of many ancient mystics. Such science does not postulate the existence of an afterlife, but by slightly shifting the probability distribution associated with quantum events, it does offer a mechanism by which the mind can impact or influence matter, as is the case with psychokinesis, and in which ghosts, spirits and other paranormal phenomena could exert their influence upon the physical world.

Delusion

Hallucination and paranoia are mental states which can involve seeing things that are not there or the feeling that you are being watched. Carbon monoxide poisoning and mould can cause hallucinations. Once all rational explanations, including medical conditions that can trigger hallucinations, are ruled out, the argument against hallucinations is that they leave the experiencer feeling drained and confused afterwards, whereas ghost sightings don't tend to have that effect. They may leave the experiencer feeling shaken or anxious but not typically disorientated or depressed.

Power of suggestion

Paranormal beliefs can offer a sense of comfort and calm and the illusion of control. During times of personal grief and crisis, the drive to self-soothe may result in seeing, feeling and/or believing things that are irrational. For example, knocking on wood is thought to offer protection from bad luck. Studies have shown that bringing lucky charms into exams can improve results. The students believe in the power of the charm, and it is that belief and not the charm itself that boosts their performance. In much the same way, studies show that if a person is told a location is allegedly haunted, they are far more likely to report hearing or seeing things. Belief is a mighty powerful force, indeed.

Projection

There is a school of thought, pioneered by Freud, which believes that ghosts are psychological thought projections to compensate for our fear of death and the unknown. In other words, we see what we most want to see or what will comfort or reassure us, as in the case of a grieving person seeing a departed loved one.

This is one of the most common theories put forward by both sceptics and scientists to discredit the possibility of ghosts: they are real only in your imagination. The argument is that regions of the brain responsible for self-awareness and perception of location may cause you to feel a ghost-like presence. In other words, when you think there's a strange presence nearby, it's because of inaccurate spatial awareness and your brain miscalculating your body's position and thinking it must be the body of someone else. Your mind is playing tricks on you.

Residual

This theory – that ghosts are residual or trapped emotional energy that has somehow imprinted itself onto a place and which can sometimes be witnessed, heard or sensed – is explored in the first section of this book. A residual haunting typically involves hearing disembodied sounds or witnessing apparitions repeating the same activity over and over again – hearing knocking at the same time night after night, for example. They are unable to interact and have no awareness of the witness or witnesses to the haunting.

Telepathy, ESP and psychokinesis

There is a theory, first suggested in the late nineteenth century by British psychical researchers Frederic Myers and Edmund Gurney, which proposes that ghosts communicate with human beings via thought or telepathy. The problem with this theory is that you have to believe in telepathy first and in much the same way as ghosts – and although there is promising research being done right now, whether or not telepathy is real remains a controversial area.

American psychical researcher Hornell Hart coined a term in the mid-twentieth century that took this telepathy explanation a giant leap further. That term was super-ESP (extrasensory perception), and it references the alleged ability of psychics and mediums to read the minds of the living to gain information about the dead, or to precognitively sense the future or retro-cognitively see visions of the past. Again, the problem with this theory is that super-ESP is as challenging a concept to prove as ghosts.

Psychokinesis is the ability to consciously or unconsciously move objects with the power of the mind alone. It is often put forward as an explanation for poltergeist hauntings, and this theory, and the arguments for and against, is explored fully in the Poltergeist section of this book.

Multiverse

The theory that all over the world there are portals or doorways to another dimension which ghosts and spirits can enter, and that there are endless parallel universes, is age-old, and arguments for and against are presented in the Inhuman section of this book. Another out-of-this-world but impossible to verify idea is that ghosts might be the result of time travel or time loops. If time is non-linear, fluctuations in time and space might offer us the opportunity to glimpse the past and the future. Beam me up, Scotty!

OBEs

Out-of-body experiences (OBEs) occur when a person's consciousness in a meditative or unconscious state allegedly leaves their body and witnesses what they could not witness in their material form. In a near-death experience (NDE), a person on the brink of death reports astonishing out-of-body visions of the afterlife.

Although there is ongoing research into NDEs, spearheaded by leading resuscitation expert Dr Sam Parnia, which has tentatively proved that one in five people who receive CPR following a cardiac arrest describe lucid experiences of death, scientists strongly disagree as to whether OBEs can be put forward as potential proof of survival. The majority believe that they are a result of neurological and psychological disturbances. Near-death experiencers, however – and I've interviewed hundreds of them – fiercely refute this, with many dramatically changing their lives and entirely losing their fear of death after this transformative experience.

To date, NDEs remain the most promising potential evidence that life after death may exist. Research in that area by scientists is ongoing. Alongside this, a whole new world of visionary scientists are diligently researching the nature of consciousness, the inner world of dreams, memories, thoughts and feelings, and the possibility of the survival of consciousness after bodily death.

True spirits

The classic or traditional view of ghosts is that they are the spirits of dead people who for some reason have got 'stuck' between this life and the next. Some of them may not even know they are dead. Some may know they are dead, however, and want to interact with the living. These are intentional hauntings and are explored in the final section of this book, on Intelligent hauntings.

Naturally occurring energy, electricity or magnetism

Everything is composed of energy, and when someone dies, their energy carries on in some form or invisible world and can be tapped into by living persons sensitive enough to perceive them. So-called ley lines (intersections said to be supercharged with supernatural energy) or natural vibrations of the earth act as magnets for energy-based manifestations and paranormal activity. This may explain why most hauntings happen at night between 9 p.m. and 3 a.m. When it is dark, there is much less resistance to every kind of magnetic and electrical current or force because the atmosphere is liberated from the bombarding solar rays of the sun.

Fraud

And then, of course, there is the argument forever put forward that ghosts are nothing more than a distortion of the truth – either a deliberate fraud or an unconscious exaggeration because a ghost story is much more exciting/lucrative than the truth. The line between fact and fiction becomes blurred over time and innocent events or illusions are misinterpreted.

Research has shown that when various parts of the brain are stimulated, visual, auditory and tactile perceptions can be disturbed, and various drugs, frequencies of sound, electrical fields, and mental and physical conditions produce hallucinations. People with schizophrenia, for example, can report seeing things that are not there, as can those going through radiotherapy or diagnosed with dementia. Although this theory is credible, applying it to all cases of haunting is unsatisfying, as in many cases the experiencer is not suffering from a physical or mental illness. It also does not explain cases where more than one person sees the phenomena. The term 'mass hysteria' is often used in this case, but again it is not a satisfying explanation in all cases, given individual behaviour is not always dictated by the dynamics of the group.

There are certainly many theories, and much more research needs to be done; there is some way to go before there is enough evidence to suggest ghosts really do exist. What is certain, though, from the countless reports of hauntings over the centuries, is that seeing or sensing ghosts is something humans experience. Ghosts, whether they are real or not, have always been with us, and until definitive proof is found to suggest that they do not exist, they are not going anywhere.

PARANORMAL POSSIBILITIES

The number 101 was chosen as a way to present the entries in this book for a specific symbolic reason. In George Orwell's classic novel *1984*, Room 101 is a prison chamber where an inmate's worst fears are manifested. And for almost all of us, the possibility of seeing a ghost when the lights go out is right up there as one of our greatest fears.

In the 101 ghost stories that follow, you will notice a number of out-of-this-world explanations being showcased. These will range from hauntings being created by imprinted energy, to kinetic energy created by the living, to psychokinesis (think Eleven moving objects with her mind in *Stranger Things*), to portals to alternative realities, to demons, to possible afterlife communication. Bear in mind that however compelling these theories may appear, at this time they remain just that: fascinating theories. Just because the science isn't quite there yet when it comes to proving that ghosts exist, that doesn't mean it will always remain that way.

It's an oversimplification, of course, but modern physics

fundamentally tells us that everything is made up of vibrating strings of interconnected infinite energy, and how this energy vibrates is how it manifests in the world. Our bodies, our feelings and our thoughts consist of energy too, so is it unfeasible to think that when we die, the energy of our thoughts and our hearts can survive in another dimension and interact with us here on earth?

From a spiritualist perspective, when we die, our spirits, the energy of our thoughts and feelings, our essence or personality, lives on, and it is this part of us that can reach back into the physical world. Countless people have written to me saying they believe they have been visited in some way by the spirit of a departed loved one, and in most cases these spirits have appeared through dreams, visions or afterlife signs to comfort, guide or simply say one last goodbye, if saying goodbye wasn't possible when they were alive. Strictly speaking, these reassuring afterlife signs are spiritual experiences rather than ghostly encounters. They comfort the bereaved with the empowering message that physical death ends a life and not a relationship, whereas ghosts typically haven't found peace on the other side. However, the distinction between ghost and spirit remains fuzzy, and any kind of communication with the other side could technically be described as haunting.

As far as mediumship or the ability to communicate with the departed is concerned, a dedicated group of pioneering scientists are actively investigating whether reliable information communicated by mediums is the result of fraud, wishful thinking, telepathy or a genuine reflection of some extended reach of consciousness. Again, studies where mediums are tested under strict scientifically controlled conditions are indicating promising results. And this research also studies the brains of mediums who consistently report accurate results when all possibility of fraud or cold reading is removed.

According to a group of pioneering parapsychologists, some people are naturally predisposed to having ghostly experiences, and there is a campaign for mental health professionals to take reports of paranormal experiences and so-called haunted people syndrome more seriously. It is thought that people who identify as highly sensitive (score highly on intuition, creativity and empathy) may be more likely to interpret anomalous events as ghostly. Wherever you lie on the sensitivity scale, however, the potential for such experiences lies within everyone; those lower on the scale may even find that episodes of emotional intensity can become a catalyst for a psychic awakening.

Afterlife research is still in its infancy but the fact that scientists are becoming more open to the idea of life after death, or at the very least willing to investigate the possibility and offer a deeper understanding of the further reaches of human consciousness, is a huge leap of faith. So much of this research is hidden in academic journals and obscured by jargon, but when you follow it and alongside it read witness statement after witness statement, it is very hard to believe that there is no credible evidence or data out there for the possibility of an afterlife at all. Of course, there is no hardcore or definitive proof that ghosts exist (yet), but equally – to risk repeating myself to stress the point – there is no hardcore or definitive proof that they don't.

So, in the spirit of quantum science, perhaps ghosts are an infinite possibility we have yet to understand fully.

ELEVEN SIGNS OF HAUNTING

Here are eleven of the most common signs of a ghostly presence. They aren't by any means the only signs, but they are more likely to occur than others. Each of these haunting signs may have a very simple, rational explanation, so we all need to think critically about all possible alternatives before assuming we've encountered a ghost.

Being watched

This is perhaps the most commonly reported sign: the sensation that you are not alone and are being stared at or watched by some kind of 'presence', or that someone is standing behind you but when you turn around, no one is there. This can occur in a specific location, like your bedroom while you are falling asleep, but it can happen to you at any time.

Invisible sensations

This sign is something you can't actually see, but you can feel it touch you, either physically or emotionally. If you have feelings of inexplicable sadness or anxiety in a certain location or in a particular room in your home, and these feelings subside when you leave that place, there is the possibility that this may not be to do with the location or your mental state. There could, and I stress *could*, be a ghostly presence lurking there.

A New York State court ruled that a seller must inform a potential buyer if their house has a history of haunting, because if they don't and the buyer discovers the history of the house, they may have to return the deposit. This is exactly what owner Helen Ackley discovered in 1991 when her potential buyer, Wall Street trader Jeffrey Stambovsky, discovered that the $650,000 Victorian house in Nyack, New York, which he had put a $3,000 deposit on, had a reputation for being haunted that dated back to the American Revolution. The court ruled that it was impossible for Stambovsky to know about the ghosts and Ackley had a duty of care to inform him.

Odours

Odours that don't seem to have any source are another potential sign. Vanilla, flowers and perfume are the most commonly reported. There is an olfactory condition called phantosmia, or smelling things that aren't there, so of course this, together with possible hidden sources of certain smells, needs to be ruled out before you consider any ghostly blame. Sometimes the odour in a haunting can be less attractive, like tobacco.

Electricity

Flickering lights or lights turning off and on by themselves or sudden flashes of bright light could be a sign. Some people believe that ghosts communicate using the invisible medium of electricity.

Ghosts in the machine

Phones or laptops may inexplicably lose battery even though they are plugged in. Your remote may not work even though the batteries are live. Your TV may switch on and off for no reason. Clocks may stop and start. Mobiles may behave erratically or send random texts. Again, there are lots of logical explanations here, such as faulty sockets and wiring, so these need to be ruled out first.

Whispers and sounds

You may hear whispers or the sound of someone calling your name, most typically on waking, but there is no source. You may also hear unexpected sounds such as footsteps or knocking sounds.

Cold spots

There might be distinct temperature drops in your home, or you may experience a sudden chill. Cold spots without any logical explanation are often said to be a sign of a haunting.

Shadow people

You may glimpse flickering figures and movement in the corner of your eye or in the mirror, but when you look closely there is nothing there. You may also notice a shadow that has no source. Shadow people are sinister and often human-shaped, and they are believed to be ghosts in dark-matter form or interdimensional beings – or something else entirely.

Signs

You may experience 'signs' that convince you a departed loved one is close by. The most commonly reported afterlife signs include the unexpected appearance of white feathers, rainbows, coins with personally significant dates on them, familiar songs and so on, just at the right moment to bring much-needed comfort.

Objects moving from place to place when you haven't touched them, or finding things in the most unlikely places, like your mobile in the fridge, could be another sign. We know that objects don't typically move on their own, so it goes without saying you need to rule out draughts, your own forgetfulness and the pranks of others first.

More than a dream

You may wake up in the middle of the night from a strange kind of dream you have not had before. Sleep paralysis and sleep disorders need to be ruled out before deciding you have been visited by ghosts. Also, we know that vivid nightmares can be triggered by stress.

Animals and nature

If you own a pet and they act alarmed around a certain location or area in your house or keep staring at a certain spot for unfathomable reasons, they could possibly be seeing something you can't. Similarly, wild animals may act in an unusual way in areas with ghostly vibrations.

You'll notice that some ghostly signs are subtle, while others are more standout. Chances are you have experienced some of the subtler signs, like a vivid dream of a departed loved one or the feeling of not being alone in a location, but not paid any attention to it before because it felt so everyday. Apparitions and objects flying through the air are as exceedingly rare as full-blown ghostly visions. From now on, if you do experience any of the subtler signs like the above, please don't be afraid. Pay closer attention. Keep a record. Write down everything you can recall about it.

STRANGER THINGS

If you wake up in the middle of the night and feel anxious in the darkness, that's OK. You are human, and centuries ago that natural-born anxiety could well have saved your life from threatening predators. Take a deep breath, sit up, switch a night light on, drink a glass of water and write your experience down in a journal. Your story can add to the ever-increasing database of strange but true happenings that parapsychologists and researchers like myself need to analyse to help us better understand these experiences. You are always welcome to share your stories with me and ask me any questions about your experiences (details on how to get in touch can be found on page 281).

Of course, when you suspect a haunting, it is always advisable to first think critically and try to eliminate the reasonable, tangible explanations before jumping to a ghostly conclusion. For example, if you feel a sudden draught, is there a window open somewhere? If you hear a strange noise every night coming from your basement, have you checked the pipes? But when you have done your due diligence and simply can't think of any other possible cause, rest assured there is no harm at all in suspecting that 'something else' might be going on. And never forget that it doesn't have to be alarming unless you allow it to be. Most ghosts are benign or unaware of your presence. The living will always be scarier than the dead.

And if 'something else' does happen to you, or what you uncover in the pages that follow opens your mind as it has never been opened before to the possibility of the world being a little stranger than you previously gave it credit for, take comfort and confidence from the knowledge that you are most certainly not alone – in more ways than one. You are in the majority. More people believe in ghosts than you might think. And if you encounter those who feel the need to belittle your openness to the possibility of an afterlife, here's a resilient quote from Swiss psychiatrist Carl Jung, from his 1919 address to the Society for Psychical Research: 'I shall not commit the fashionable stupidity of dismissing everything I cannot explain as fraud.'

So, armed with your new-found illumination when the lights go out, it's time to plunge headfirst into a whirlwind tour of 101 well-reported cases of hauntings from around the globe.

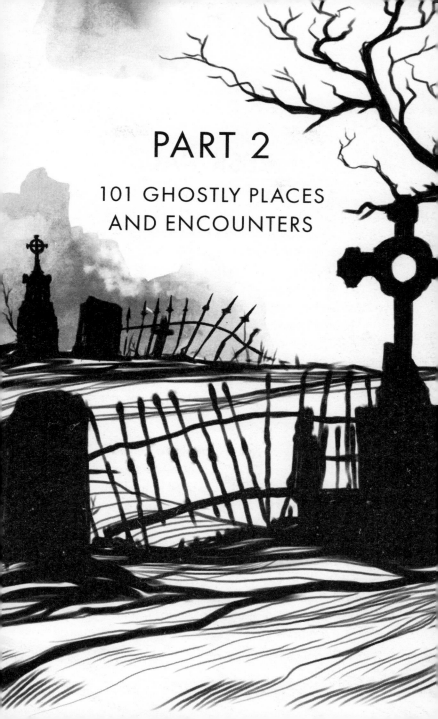

PART 2

101 GHOSTLY PLACES AND ENCOUNTERS

RESIDUAL

'The wind was trying to whisper something to me and I couldn't make out what it was, and so it made the cold shivers run over me. Then away out in the woods I heard that kind of a sound that a ghost makes when it wants to tell about something that's on its mind and can't make itself understood, and so can't rest easy in its grave and has to go about that way every night grieving.'

The Adventures of Huckleberry Finn,
Mark Twain

Residual hauntings remain the most commonly reported paranormal activity. However, some parapsychologists don't actually believe they should be classified as hauntings.

A residual haunting may be a recording or an imprint of a person, scene, sound, smell or image that is inexplicably on a loop and keeps repeating itself. It is like a living memory. They are often reported in places where a traumatic or tragic event has happened and the energy of that event has somehow imprinted. That's why battlefields or crime scenes are often locations for these kinds of hauntings. However, in some instances, residuals are created by the release of energy from a repetitive event or action that took place there – repeated knocking or rapping on a door, for example, or creaks on a frequently used staircase.

The haunting can be visual but is more likely to involve inexplicable footsteps, sounds, whispers or scents. There is no consciousness involved – so in that sense they are not technically 'ghosts' or 'spirits' – and if there is any interaction with the environment, it is said to be due to the imprinted energy expanding. Apparitions will be witnessed in the same locations doing the same things, perhaps walking in the same room or area. They won't be aware of living people or anything around them. They may walk through walls or even people. They are trapped in their own never-ending past.

In essence, energetic impressions reveal themselves in a residual haunting, like a repeated memory that you can see, hear or smell but can't interact with. No one knows why or how these hauntings are triggered, but there are, of course, theories. For instance, there are more reports of residuals during the colder winter months, when there is more static electricity, and during storms, so temperature and atmosphere changes could be a catalyst. Artificial energy sources and electricity currents may also be a factor. The moon's energy impacts the tides, so perhaps lunar vibrations can ignite hauntings too. And it has also been suggested that under the right conditions the earth's electromagnetic fields somehow act like a recorder.

Places identified with violence and trauma are often subject to residual hauntings. For instance, the term 'grey lady' (or 'white lady' if she is seen wearing white rather than grey) is often used by paranormal researchers to describe the ghost of a woman who died broken-hearted or who was killed by someone she knew. Grey ladies have been reported all over the world, but some of the most well-known are associated with the British Tudor period, perhaps because at the time ladies who made indiscretions were sent to nunneries, where the habits worn were grey.

It is also thought that scenes of intense emotion – like battlefields, for example – can imprint themselves on the surrounding atmosphere as the ghosts of those who died abruptly can't find peace. Others believe retrocognition – vividly sensing the past – is an element of such hauntings. Paranormal investigators who believe hauntings can be caused by the consciousness of the living often use battlefield hauntings to support their case. The theory is that the anguish a war causes imprints itself on collective memory and hauntings are a way of keeping alive the memory and lessons learned from such a tragic waste of life. Retrocognition is sometimes offered as an explanation for residual hauntings more generally. It is suggested that a psychic or highly sensitive person can somehow tune into the frequency of that residual energy and 'see' or 'feel' it, though there is no proof of this theory yet.

Stone Tape theory is the also unproven but often cited idea that the age of a building and the vast number of people it has seen and the amount of history that has happened there may somehow prompt the saving or recording of impressions, images and sounds from the past. And materials used in very old buildings may have properties that can absorb, retain and release energy. One of those properties may be the amount of water in the structure. Some scientists believe water can retain memories of substances or energy it has mixed with. Bricks are made up of at least 10 per cent water, so perhaps the water within bricks can trap a memory, not to mention that humans consist of up to 70 per cent water. Water can conduct electricity, so perhaps it can also conduct paranormal activity.

Humidity levels and the amount of water within and around a location could therefore be key. Many residuals are reported by lakes, rivers or underground water sources.

Moving pictures

A defining characteristic of residuals is that they are unconscious of the present moment. If an apparition is involved, it will be like watching a movie projector image on a loop that vanishes as soon as the witness attempts to approach or converse with it. The same applies to non-visual residual hauntings. At any attempt by the witness to engage, the mysterious repeated sounds, noises, voices and smells discontinue, leaving the witness wondering if they were imagining it all. The argument against it all being a figment of the imagination is if other people unconnected to each other and at different times experienced something similar.

For this reason, should you ever experience or decide to investigate the scene of an alleged residual haunting, it is essential that you keep a written record, or better still a video recording or photographic image, of anything you witness or experience. The place, the position and the timing of the haunting all matter greatly. As a budding citizen parapsychologist/scientist investigating the paranormal, you need reliable evidence that is time and date-stamped.

Although residuals are often spontaneous, making it impossible in many cases to keep a video or photographic record, you can always ensure you create written 'proof' immediately afterwards. This is not just to see if you can detect a pattern or a potential explanation but to remind yourself that what you witnessed or experienced really did happen.

And so, without further ado, it is high time now to begin your induction into the hall of some well-reported residual hauntings.

1. HEATHROW AIRPORT

If you imagine a haunted location, your thoughts will probably gravitate towards ancient, eerie, deserted and creepy places, not a modern, noisy, bustling airport. Yet Heathrow Airport, the main international airport serving London, is consistently named as one of the UK's most haunted locations according to online searches. And for good reason.

A mysterious apparition of an anxious-looking businessman wearing a dark suit and a bowler hat and fruitlessly searching for his briefcase is said to haunt the runways. The briefcase man's haunting history dates back to a foggy March night in 1948, when an incoming Belgian Airlines DC3 Dakota plane nosedived, crashed and exploded at Heathrow, which was then called London Airport. At least seventeen people, including three crew, were killed as the plane burst into flames when it hit the ground, with only five surviving.

According to reports, the plane had warned the airport that it needed to make an emergency landing. Emergency services arrived speedily at the scene, with firefighters and paramedics battling unsuccessfully against the intense heat and thick fog to save the victims. The skeletal inside of the plane was like an inferno. Anguished screams could be heard from inside the aircraft as passengers struggled to unbuckle their seat belts inside the burning plane. Many burned to death on the runway. Despite this, firefighters bravely battled foam, ashes, debris and flames for hours to try to search for survivors. The fog and mud were major impediments to the rescue operation, with the headlights of the ambulances and fire engines required on full blast to light their way. The few passengers who were rescued were taken to a nearby hospital with critical injuries. Eventually the fire burned out, leaving only parts of the wing and tailplane.

Considering the plane had crashed dangerously close to houses nearby on the Bath Road, the loss of life could have been much worse. Although this wasn't reported in the press at the time, the story goes that several of the rescue workers afterwards mentioned a man who emerged from the wreckage asking them if anyone had seen his briefcase. As they made their way towards him, he vanished. When it later came to searching the wreckage, the body of the very same man was found inside.

The ghost of the man looking for his briefcase – and whose body was found dead in the wreckage – has been sighted many times since, with one remarkable report documented in 1970, when the airport's radar office picked up a signal which looked like a person on the runaway. Police rushed to the spot, but when they arrived on the scene there was no one in sight.

The stressed businessman theme continues with another ghost believed to haunt the VIP lounges. He is said to wear a grey suit and sometimes to appear as just a pair of legs!

Airline staff at the main terminal have also reported feeling warm breath on their necks, as well as what sounds like a howling dog, but when they turn around there is nobody there. This is said to be none other than notorious Georgian highwayman Dick Turpin, who allegedly loved to howl behind people's backs or blow on their necks as a prank when he was alive. He was hanged for his crimes in 1739. For some reason, his ghost is believed to frequent the airport and is said to have haunted the grounds even before the terminal was built.

Airports are tense enough places without adding a potential ghost investigation into the mix. And don't restrict yourself to the airport interior alone: a substantial Neolithic settlement is thought to have once occupied the vicinity of Heathrow, with artefacts found in the gravel around the airport.

2. WAVERLY HILLS SANATORIUM

Dr Ian Stevenson, an American clinical psychiatrist and the founder and director of the Division of Perceptual Studies at the University of Virginia School of Medicine, caused quite a stir in the media when he boldly stated that hauntings could no longer, in his opinion, be dismissed entirely as hallucination or hoax. He argued that 'evidence for these kinds of experiences are too frequent to be dismissed'.

The fact that many sanatoriums and hospitals are well-known places for ghost stories is perhaps no surprise, given they witness their fair share of trauma, mental illness and untimely death. But the sanatorium that sits atop Waverly Hills in Louisville, Kentucky, is perhaps one of the most notorious and well reported.

Waverly has a grim, Gothic design. If you were to direct a movie about a haunted asylum, this building would probably be your inspiration. Construction dates back to 1910, and it was built to treat victims of the terrible plague that was wiping out entire communities at the time. This disease, known as the 'white death', was tuberculosis. Kentucky, being built on low swampland, was particularly badly impacted with damp, making the city a breeding ground for disease. Antibiotics had not yet been discovered and there was no cure, so isolating the infected was considered to be the best option. The contagious, whether wealthy or poor, were all encouraged to seek 'healthy air' in sanatoriums.

Most who contracted the white death and were sent to Waverly died. The building became notorious for the number of desperate medical treatments doctors experimented with there, most of which were as deadly as the disease itself. One involved seriously ill and weak patients being placed in front of open windows or on the roof – regardless of how hot or cold it was – to be 'treated' by fresh air. Another involved the surgical implantation of balloons in the lungs that were then filled with blood and air in an attempt to enable oxygen flow. In an even grislier procedure, patients had muscles and ribs removed in an attempt to give their lungs more room to fill with air. Unsurprisingly this often had disastrous results, and many patients did not survive.

Historians suggest that the white death claimed at least 6,000 lives at Waverly Sanatorium, although rumours circulate of there being thousands more. Those few who did survive left through the front door, but the majority who didn't make it were removed through the 'body chute', an underground death tunnel that extended to the railroad tracks and was used to transport the dead away from the hospital so that the living could not see them.

The sanatorium was closed in 1961, but a year later it reopened until 1982 as Woodhaven Geriatric Center. The disturbing experimental medical spirit remained, with alarming reports of patients being used as guinea pigs for electroshock treatments. Between 1983 and 2001 the building was abandoned but frequently broken into by homeless people and vandals. During this time the hospital began to garner a reputation for being haunted, with reports of apparitions of a woman with bleeding wrists screaming in agony, hearses manifesting at the rear of the building and dropping off coffins, and ghost children running up and down stairs. There were also accounts of lights switching on and off when the building had no electricity, footsteps, doors creaking shut, and the smell of cooking and bread-making coming from the kitchen that was no longer in use.

Room 502, however, remains the topic of most fascination for ghost hunters. The fifth floor consists of two nurses' areas, a medical room, a bedsheet room and two dorms. There have been many reports by visitors to Room 502 of shapes in the windows and disembodied voices telling them to 'leave' or 'get out'. Room 502 is believed to have been the scene of a double tragedy. In

1928, a pregnant, unmarried nurse is reported to have hanged herself from the light fixture, where her body was not discovered for several days. Another nurse who worked in the same room is thought to have taken her own life by jumping off the roof in 1932, plunging to her death. Her reasons for doing so are unknown, and even today rumours persist that she may actually have been pushed. There is no proof or evidence to back up the stories, but nevertheless the room has a grisly reputation.

Since 2001, Waverly Hills has become a paranormal tour attraction, with proceeds going towards ongoing restoration. There have been multiple investigations of the sanatorium by professional ghost hunters as well as an endless stream of curious visitors who report sightings of apparitions and unexplained noises in the dark.

3. THE LONDON UNDERGROUND

Every year, the London Underground transports millions of passengers, but whether you are a believer or a sceptic, only the bravest would want to spend a night alone in an empty Tube train or carriage. If reports are to be believed, you may not be entirely alone down there. Dating back to January 1863 with the Metropolitan Railway, the world's first underground passenger railway, the Tube has lashings of reported paranormal activity. Here are just a few chilling examples.

Aldgate station was built on top of a site used to bury bodies during the deadly 1665 Great Plague, and strange moans have been reported by passengers there. It also boasts a reported sighting of an apparition of a woman who is believed to have been electrocuted there during the Second World War. The story goes that an electrician was electrocuted while working on the tracks, but despite the shock, he survived. His colleagues told him they were convinced they saw a woman stroking his hair moments before he was electrocuted.

Less than a mile down the road, a bomb fell from a German aircraft onto Bank station on 11 January 1942. It killed over fifty people, and since then reports of anguished screams have been heard when the station is quiet. However, Bank's most famous ghost dates back to the nineteenth century. She is said to be the ghost of Sarah Whitehead. Sarah's brother worked for the Bank of England but was executed for fraud in 1812, the trauma of which sent his sister mad. For years afterwards, she would visit the bank dressed in her mourning clothes asking to see her brother. A wandering woman in black weeping loudly has been spotted by both staff and commuters in various areas of the station. She is sometimes referred to ominously as the Black Nun.

Covent Garden station also seems to have a resident ghost. There have been several sightings by station staff of a gentleman in Victorian attire with opera cape, top hat and elegant white gloves who drifts along the platforms and tunnels, as well as lights switching on and off by themselves and unexplained rapping sounds. It is thought that this may be the ghost of a beloved Victorian melodramatic actor, William Terriss. He was known as 'Breezy Bill' due to his charisma and because he always played the hero. Tragically, he was murdered by a paranoid fellow actor called Richard Prince at the stage door of the Adelphi Theatre in 1897. The murder caused a press sensation at the time, especially as he was said to have died in the arms of his distraught leading lady uttering the last words: 'I will come back.' Those who have reported sightings of the resident ghost have identified him as Terriss when later shown pictures of the actor.

Farringdon station's ghost (also known as the Screaming Spectre) dates back to 1758, when a teenage girl was brutally murdered and her body dumped near where the Tube station now stands. Ann Nailor has never been spotted physically, but both passengers and staff have allegedly heard her disembodied screams echoing in the darkness of the tunnels. Another ghost who is heard but never seen is the Elephant and Castle station 'runner'. In the early hours of the morning, station staff have reported unexplained running sounds coming and going and then abruptly stopping, as well as strange tappings and slamming doors. There have also been reports of an unknown woman boarding a northbound train before mysteriously disappearing behind the closing doors.

4. THE *QUEEN MARY*

Luxury ocean liner the *Queen Mary* first set sail in May 1936 and swiftly gained a reputation as the gold standard of international travel. During the Second World War she underwent a dramatic transformation into a vessel to transport troops, and her final voyage was in October 1967, after which she ended up docked permanently at Long Beach, California. This time her transformation was into a floating hotel.

Although unsinkable during the war, the *Queen Mary* was no stranger to tragedy and subsequent reports of haunting, apparently the site of almost fifty deaths during her time at sea and now playing host to over 100 ghosts. In 1966, an eighteen-year-old engine room worker called John Pedder was crushed to death by automatic hatch No. 13. A figure with grease marks on his face that look like fingerprints has been seen whistling in the area and wandering the hallways. But perhaps the ship's most notorious ghost is a cook called Leonard 'Lobster', who served on the ship for fifteen years and died of heart failure on her final voyage in 1967. His body was buried at sea, but it is said that his ghost remains on board and makes his presence felt in the kitchen area.

Another ghost that has been reported on board is that of a man in white overalls. He is believed to have been an engineer who worked on the ship in the 1930s. There are also reports of a pale woman in a white backless evening dress who floats close to the grand piano, dances for a few moments and then vanishes.

In 1948, Stateroom B340 was the scene of the death of a British third-class passenger called Walter Adamson. The cause of Adamson's death is unknown, but a woman who stayed in the room in 1966 reported that she was woken up by a man standing at the foot of her bed. When she screamed for the steward, the man disappeared from sight. In the years since, guests in this room have reported a mysterious knocking and lights turning on and off. Maids have reported the bathroom taps inexplicably running when no one is staying in the room. Stateroom B340 became so infamous for its ghosts that it was closed to guests for many years before being opened as a haunted attraction, and now some crew members still refuse to go inside – including, according to some reports, the ship's current captain.

Two maids were also terrified in 1989 when they went to clean the Mauretania lounge. They both saw a passenger sitting alone and still like a statue on a chair in the middle of the dance floor, staring at them – but when they called security, the passenger vanished right in front of their eyes.

In 2001, an employee working in the Mayfair room, the ship's former beauty salon area, arrived early for work at around 5.30 a.m. Alone in the room, she reported feeling unusually cold and that someone had brushed up against her chair before she noticed an apparition of a transparent person in white walking across the room and right through the door. The now-abandoned swimming pool area is also believed to be a hotbed of paranormal activity, with sightings of a woman in a Gothic-looking wedding gown, a little boy in a suit and a little girl in a blue dress who all disappear when spotted. Boiler Room 4 also has reports of a little girl holding a doll and sucking her thumb.

In addition to ghosts that are seen, heard or felt, visitors, staff and security workers have all reported unexplained incidents, such as alarms triggering by themselves and doors opening and closing for no reason. Inexplicable draughts, cold spots, disembodied voices, footsteps, lights switching on and off, and strange bangs and noises complete the ghostly repertoire.

5. HAMPTON COURT PALACE

Located in Surrey, England, Hampton Court Palace was built in the early sixteenth century by Cardinal Thomas Wolsey before being passed to King Henry VIII, who renovated it in keeping with his lavish style.

Henry's fifth wife, Catherine Howard, was beheaded for adultery and treason. When she was arrested at Hampton Court at the tender age of nineteen, she tried to run away from the guards into what is now called the haunted gallery. She screamed repeatedly during her futile escape attempt for Henry to show her mercy, but the King refused to see her. She was dragged away to her death by the guards. However, her ghost appears to have remained in the palace, making the same tragic journey to the gallery over and over again. Visitors to the haunted gallery have reported feeling inexplicably cold, and in

1999, two women on two different tours of the palace fainted in exactly the same spot.

Rumour has it that Henry's third wife, Jane Seymour, also haunts the palace. She was perhaps his favourite wife because she gave birth to his much longed for and only son, who later became King Edward VI. Jane died from post-birth complications in 1537, twelve days after giving birth to Edward. Jane's pale and mournful figure, wearing white and carrying a candle, has been spotted on a number of occasions on the anniversary of Edward's birth, 12 October, on the Silverstick stairs, which are a passage to the room where Jane gave birth.

As well as Henry's distraught wives, a so-called grey lady is believed to linger at Hampton Court. She is thought to have been a loyal nursemaid to Edward VI and Elizabeth I, called Sybil Penn. She caught smallpox from Elizabeth and was buried in a nearby church until her tomb was disturbed due to church renovations in around the 1830s. Ever since, she has been spotted wandering aimlessly in the corridors, sometimes carrying a baby in her arms. Residents at the palace in the early 1800s also reported the whirring sound of a spinning wheel behind the wall of their apartment, though it wasn't until later that a small sealed chamber was discovered, containing nothing but an old, well-used spinning wheel.

In 1871, a resident of the palace complained of banging on her walls that disturbed her sleep, but she was not taken seriously. Soon afterwards, the skeletons of two males were found in unknown graves adjacent to her rooms – and once the skeletons were given a proper burial, the banging stopped. It has been suggested that the two men were killed in the civil wars and hastily buried in unmarked graves that were built over when the baroque parts of the palace were constructed.

In winter 2003, CCTV footage that drew considerable media attention captured a skeletal, ghostly figure in a heavy-hooded robe bursting through a set of fire doors in the palace, violently throwing the doors back and looking out into the courtyard before disappearing back into the shadows. On three consecutive days security staff were called to close one particular door near the palace's Clock Court. The ghostly figure appeared on the second day, and it wasn't just the security guards who saw him: on the same day, a visitor noted in the guestbook that she had seen a spectral figure in the same area.

Security guards back then and to this day can't explain the mystery of who or what this was. The incident can still be viewed online, with the terrifying figure earning itself the eerie nickname 'Skeletor'. Check it out and make your own mind up. Prank or a true ghost? You decide.

6. CHÂTEAU DE BRISSAC

Built during the eleventh century by the Counts of Anjou, Château de Brissac is the tallest castle in France. At seven storeys high, when you gaze at its splendour your eyes soar upwards. Located in Maine-et-Loire, like many castles it has a lengthy and sumptuous history, complete with its very own resident ghost.

The Green Lady of Château de Brissac is believed to be the ghost of Charlotte de Brézé, who was the illegitimate daughter of King Charles VII and his mistress Agnes Sorel and the beloved half-sister of Louis XI. A politically motivated marriage was arranged in 1462 between Charlotte and Jacques de Brézé, a nobleman. The two were a very poor match; they could barely tolerate being in each other's company and did not sleep in the same bedroom. One night, a servant woke Jacques up to inform him that his wife was having an affair with a huntsman called Pierre de Lavergne. Jacques burst into their bedroom and caught the two of them in a passionate embrace. In a fit of rage, he killed them both. Accounts differ here, as one version suggests that Jacques killed the couple with a hundred deadly blows of his sword, while another version states that he strangled Charlotte in the Chapel Tower. Either way, it is almost certain that he killed them both, and neither was ever seen again.

Jacques was evicted from the château soon afterwards. He spent time in prison, but his life was eventually spared by Louis XI when he gave all his property to the Crown. It was rumoured that Jacques spent the rest of his days haunted by strange moans, believed to be the ghosts of his wife and her lover.

For centuries there have been reports of Charlotte's apparition at the castle by the resident family. She appears to haunt the place where her life was so violently taken by her husband, and while Pierre's ghost seems to have departed the residence, the

Green Lady has been spotted by witnesses on numerous occasions wearing a flowing green dress in the tower room of the chapel. Alarmingly, there are large holes where her nose and eyes should be, suggesting this is how her mutilated body was found after her murder. As well as sightings when darkness falls, visitors to the château have reported hearing strange moans, gentle footsteps and the occasional disembodied burst of laughter.

The Green Lady is perhaps the most famous ghost story in France. Her sad and terrifying tale of betrayal, jealousy, love and passion among the nobility continues to capture the imagination and keep her restless spirit alive as tourists flock to this splendid castle.

7. THE ANCIENT RAM INN

Did you know that there is a building in England which is believed to be so haunted, so alive with menacing spirits, that some local residents to this day refuse even to walk past it at night? That building is called the Ancient Ram Inn and is located in scenic Wotton-under-Edge, Gloucestershire, England.

The inn was built on the site of an ancient burial ground from 5,000 years ago, and some believe the redirection of water during the building process opened up a portal that allowed ghosts to filter through. Evidence of pagan sacrifice has also been found at the inn, with ancient broken daggers found in the excavation of a grave of the skeletal remains of a woman and child. A former Bishop of Gloucester, the Rt Rev. John Yates, allegedly tried to exorcise the Ancient Ram and is quoted in the local press as saying it was one of the 'most evil places' he had ever had the 'misfortune to visit'.

Others suggest that the inn resides on not just one but two ley lines. Visitors to the inn have reported the distressing sounds of babies crying or felt invisible forces pushing them when they walk upstairs. A photograph taken in June 1999 reveals white mist that vaguely resembles a human form ascending the staircase.

The bishop's room on the first floor is said to be the most disturbing. Two monks have been seen appearing and disappearing in that room, as has the apparition of a cavalier who materializes by the dressing table and strides purposefully across the room. There are also reports of anguished screaming, believed to be that of a man who was murdered by having his head pushed into a fire in this doomed room. And there's more. A ghostly shepherd and his sheep dog also visit the room from time to time, and those who spent the night in there when the inn was still a bed and breakfast were so plagued by nightmares that they often refused to spend another night in the room.

The attic was the scene of the murder of an innkeeper's daughter in the early 1500s. People visiting the bishop's room below have heard the sound of what could be a body being dragged across the floor of the empty attic. Climbing up into the roof, visitors are greeted by a feeling of intense melancholy.

Other sightings include the apparition of a woman who was burned at the stake for witchcraft in the 1500s – it is said that this woman hid in a room now called the 'Witch's Room' before her arrest, torture and execution – and a ghostly centurion on horseback, who terrified a plumber working at the inn when the apparition rode right through the walls. And the terror continues outside the inn too, as in the old barn, tall, looming shadows have been seen and, in some cases, people witnessing them have temporarily felt paralysed by fear.

The Ancient Ram Inn is open to the public and a favourite location for ghost hunters. Those brave enough to enter describe the atmosphere as heavy, dark and truly foul. Is this because ghosts linger there or because when you enter the inn it feels as if you are travelling back in time? With its steep stairs, twisting narrow corridors, creaking floorboards, cold spots, bare walls embedded with eerie recollections and looming shadows from the past, it is just how you would imagine a haunted residence to look and feel. Not surprisingly, it has been investigated many times by paranormal researchers and TV shows and has rightfully earned its reputation as one of the most unforgettable and sinister locations to visit in the world.

8. EASTERN STATE PENITENTIARY

Pennsylvania's Eastern State Penitentiary boasts a particularly unsavoury past. It was built in 1829 with 30 feet high walls and looks very much like a Gothic medieval stone fortress. Prisoners who were originally sent there were placed in extreme solitary confinement. The misguided justification and belief at the time was that solitude could encourage positive reflection and be a reformative process.

Doomed inmates were placed in solitary for twenty-three hours a day. They saw literally no one and were forced to wear hoods, preventing them from communicating with or even seeing their fellow inmates. In a particular act of cruelty, guards covered their shoes with fabric so prisoners couldn't hear their footsteps. Talking was emphatically not allowed, and if inmates attempted to communicate with each other by tapping on pipes, the punishments were severe. It was unimaginable physical and psychological torture, and perhaps the pain and the madness somehow imprinted themselves. Indeed, the term 'penitentiary' originated with the grotesque regime so ruthlessly and enthusiastically implemented by wardens at Eastern State and the belief that prisoners would become genuinely penitent.

Throughout its history, Eastern State was riddled with corruption, mental illness, suicide, murder, cruelty, injustice, torture and disease. The prison was shut down in the early 1970s and later turned into a preserved historical building and tourist attraction, with frequent reports of alleged paranormal activity. The building has been allowed to decay naturally, making it a paranormal enthusiast's dream (or should I say nightmare) to investigate and photograph. The crumbling walls and lightless cells with steel beds make Eastern State the perfect setting for directors, with many a TV show, documentary and blockbuster movie, such as *12 Monkeys* (where Eastern State is the scene of an insane asylum), filmed there.

Over the years, both staff and visitors have reported hearing eerie howls and frantic footsteps echoing in the corridors and cells, as well as shadowy figures dancing and tortured faces momentarily appearing on the walls, with cell blocks 4, 6 and 12 believed to be particularly active as the sites of repeated reports of echoing voices, cackling and apparitions. Many visitors experience feelings of oppressive and heavy negativity that in some cases exhaust them not just emotionally but physically. They feel weak at the knees and breathless, and one staff member was even left unable to move by an unknown force that then beckoned him deeper into the cell.

9. THE TEN BELLS PUB

The Ten Bells Pub, on the corner of Commercial Street and Fournier Street in Spitalfields in London's East End, dates back to at least the 1740s. It is steeped in history and has gruesome associations with Jack the Ripper and a host of other dark deeds. No wonder it is ranked among the most haunted pubs in London.

Annie Chapman was the second victim of Jack the Ripper, a sadistic serial killer of prostitutes who terrorized the streets of London in the Victorian era, horrifically mutilating his targets. Annie drank alone for several hours in the Ten Bells before falling into his evil trap, and her traumatized ghost is believed to haunt the pub.

The Ripper's third victim, Elizabeth Stride, also frequented the pub, and his final victim, Mary Kelly, was drinking there on the night before her murder. Mysterious laughter, loud footsteps and the sensation of being touched by invisible hands have been reported by both staff and guests of the pub.

Glimpses of a man wearing Victorian attire have been reported multiple times. Often, this gentleman appears and then disappears in the upper hallway. Overnight guests have complained of nightmares, with some stating that they woke up in the middle of the night to find him lying beside them. As soon as they cry for help, he vanishes.

In 2000, the mystery of this gentleman's identity may have been solved. A box was discovered in the cellar containing items that belonged to an ex-landlord called George Roberts, who is said to have been murdered with an axe. His murderer was never brought to justice, so perhaps George's ghost is still hoping that injustice will be rectified.

The top-floor room is believed to be a paranormal hotspot. One psychic refused to enter the room and told the landlord they sensed that a baby had died there in the 1800s under disturbing circumstances. A few years later a researcher investigating the pub found a sack tucked behind a water tank in the roof containing mouldy Victorian baby clothes which had been ripped by a knife. In a creepy twist, the discovery was made directly above the room the psychic had refused to enter.

Maybe some of the reports of objects moving, unexplained cold draughts, invisible forces and apparitions spotted in the walls have something to do with what is served to customers from the Ten Bells' barrels; they may only be having a frightfully good time. Or maybe there really is something sinister and unexplained going on. Given several of his victims were found close to the Ten Bells, it is entirely possible Jack the Ripper selected and stalked his vulnerable victims there. Simply knowing that perhaps the world's most famous serial killer, whose identity remains unknown to this day, may have been a regular there is a chilling enough thought, guaranteed to give you the creeps. And many people who visit the pub say they can sense his malevolent and suffocating presence still hanging there like the heavy London smog.

10. ST AUGUSTINE LIGHTHOUSE

Hezekiah Pittee was hired to oversee the reconstruction of St Augustine Lighthouse in Florida in the early 1870s. He brought his family from their hometown in Cape Elizabeth, Maine, to live with him in Augustine so they could be close by as he worked. Pittee lived on site with his wife and their children, Mary, Eliza, Edward and Carrie. His children loved playing together with the children of other construction workers on the site. They had tremendous fun riding an old railway cart used to transport building material down to the sea; it was their homemade version of a Victorian roller coaster.

The builders, concerned for the safely of the girls, placed a wooden board on the tracks so the cart would stop before it tipped over into the water. For reasons that remain unknown, on 10 July 1873, the board was not there. Blissfully unaware of their impending doom, Mary (aged fifteen), Eliza (aged thirteen), Carrie (aged four) and an unnamed girl (aged ten) boarded the railway cart. When the cart reached the sea, it not only carried right on into the water, it also flipped over, trapping the girls inside. Workers rushed to the scene to try to lift the cart, but tragically they could only save Carrie. The other three girls died.

In the years since, there have been reports from lighthouse keepers and their families, as well as visitors, of sightings of the young girls in their Victorian attire. James Pippin, who was keeper from 1953 to 1955, moved when he became convinced the house was haunted. A local man who lived there in the 1960s stated that he woke once in the middle of the night to see a young girl standing at the foot of his bed, but when he blinked several times in an attempt to see the little girl more clearly, she vanished into thin air.

A fire badly damaged the building in the 1970s, and during construction work a number of incidents were reported, with the basement being most busy, perhaps because the children often played there when they were alive. One paranormal investigator believed that the girls may have communicated with her via an EMF recorder, used to measure electrical activity. The recorder spiked when she asked them if they wanted to play hide and seek. She went to search for them in the basement and the EMF spiked again when she looked under the stairs.

On one occasion a visitor on a lighthouse tour praised the good behaviour of another visitor's daughter she had seen stay close and silent by her mother's side. This caused everyone considerable confusion, because not only did the other visitor not have a daughter, but there were no children on that particular tour, suggesting this may have been an apparition.

On another occasion a staff member closing up for the night heard giggles at the top of the tower. Thinking there must be someone up there, he climbed to the top but found it empty. While walking back down he heard the giggles again, but again there was no one there. If you search online you can find a haunting photograph of the Pittee girls taken when they were alive.

11. THE LANGHAM HOTEL

A regular haunt of royalty, celebrities, artists, musicians and, if the sheer number of reported paranormal incidents are to be believed, ghosts, the Langham Hotel in Portland Place, London, is regarded as one of the most prestigious hotels in the world. Designed in the style of a luxurious Florentine palace, the hotel opened in 1865, and in its day it was considered thoroughly modern, offering lifts, air conditioning and other never-before-seen innovations that would go on to transform the hotel business.

During the Second World War, it became a first-aid station for soldiers after being too damaged to keep open, and then in the 1950s it was purchased by the BBC both for broadcasting and for housing BBC staff.

Reports of paranormal activity began in the 1950s BBC-owned era. These include repeated sightings of ghosts such as Napoleon III, who stayed at the Langham during his exile, a Second World War soldier who walks through walls, and a man with a grotesque gaping wound in his face stumbling through the hotel halls. There have also been sightings of a window-jumping ghost, this time believed to be a German prince who repeats his final journey over and over again. Certain areas of the hotel feel suddenly icy cold for no apparent reason. These strange things, however, pale in comparison to the distressing incidents reported on several occasions on the third floor, in particular in Room 333.

The story goes that a grey-haired Victorian doctor checked into Room 333 with his beautiful younger wife on their wedding night. Before their honeymoon ended, the not-so-good doctor violently attacked and killed his bride with a knife and then killed himself. A BBC reporter staying in Room 333 woke one night to see a ball of light gradually transform into a human form but only from the knees up. The reporter did what all good reporters do. He asked the apparition a question – what did it want? – but the apparition did not reply and instead, looking at him with vacant eyes, stretched out its arms and began to move towards him. The reporter, terrified and eager to find a witness, ran to a nearby room to get a colleague to confirm he wasn't seeing things. The colleague agreed, and when they rushed back to Room 333 they both saw the ghost briefly before it vanished from sight.

Paranormal investigations in the room have recorded strange noises and unexplained feelings of dread. Those who have stayed overnight have said they were woken up by their bed shaking. One Room 333 guest was so terrified by whatever they experienced in the room that they demanded to check out of the hotel in the middle of the night. Indeed, Room 333 now has such a haunted reputation that it is rarely rented to guests. The hotel will, however, allow you to put in a request to stay in Room 333 if you (and they) feel your constitution (and financial contribution) is strong enough.

12. THE CASTLE OF GOOD HOPE

The Castle of Good Hope was built between 1666 and 1680 by soldiers, sailors and slaves and is the oldest existing building in South Africa. Declared a historical monument in 1936, the original Dutch East India Company fortress construction of clay and timber dates back to 1650. It was built to supply ships passing the dangerous coast around the Cape, but to the indigenous people it was a gloomy symbol of their dispossession.

The fortress contains a bell tower, living quarters, a church, shops and a dungeon. During the Second Boer War from 1899 to 1902, the castle was used as a torture chamber, gallows and prison, frequently for troublesome chiefs of indigenous people.

Despite its optimistic title, the Castle of Good Hope has a sinister reputation. Disembodied voices and footsteps have been reported by both workers and visitors in the windowless dungeon and gloomy corridors. Night watchmen believe anguished souls linger in the castle archways, so they avoid that area at night.

The bell in the bell tower sometimes rings of its own accord, which is inexplicable, since it has been bricked up for decades. It is believed that the ghost of a soldier who hanged himself by the bell rope rings the bell. It's not just the old bell that is said to have a mind of its own; there's an electric bell which eerily rings out when nobody is around.

One of the castle's most infamous ghosts is believed to be that of a harsh and unforgiving former governor called Pieter Gijsbert van Noodt. On 23 April 1728, van Noodt sentenced seven men to death and refused to grant one prisoner's last wish before his hanging. That prisoner cursed him, and on the same day that prisoner was hanged, van Noodt died unexpectedly of a heart attack in his office. According to legend, he died with a look of terror and surprise on his face. Castle staff and visitors report that they can sense his cruel presence inside the castle and hear him cursing 300 years after his death.

Perhaps most ominously, the castle is also haunted by the alarming ghost of a black dog that lunges at people before vanishing. People have also witnessed what they believe to be a tall man leaping off the castle walls – before his body hits the ground, it fades and disappears. There does seem to be one ghost who is less terrifying and that is the ghost of Lady Anne Barnard, who lived at the castle towards the end of the eighteenth century. Lady Anne entertained prestigious guests when she was alive and enjoyed being a hostess so much she is said still to reappear centuries later, but only when very important guests visit.

13. RAYNHAM HALL

There are a number of allegedly haunted houses, castles and abbeys open to the public in Britain. Raynham Hall in Norfolk, however, stands out both for its association with perhaps the most famous ghost photograph of all time and also because of its reticence in showcasing its paranormal reputation.

In contrast to many sites believed to be haunted, the owners of Raynham Hall have typically preferred to downplay its paranormal reputation and focus on its stunning architecture instead. However, this may well be an impossible task, because the Brown Lady of Raynham Hall spirit photograph taken in 1936 and originally published in *Country Life* magazine can easily be viewed online. It remains the subject of great debate among ghost hunters and parapsychologists. In this photograph, you can clearly see the transparent figure of a woman with a shadowy hooded cloak wafting down the magnificent staircase of Raynham Hall.

The figure is believed to be the ghost of the eighteenth-century mistress of the manor, Lady Dorothy Walpole. Lady Dorothy, the sister of Robert Walpole, endured an unhappy marriage to Viscount Townshend at Raynham. There were rumours that she had an affair, while other rumours state her lavish spending incurred the viscount's rage. Whatever the reason, she died 'mysteriously'.

The first reported sighting of the Brown Lady dates back to 1835. Major Loftus, a visitor, claimed he saw a vision of a lady in a brown dress with sockets for eyes. Then, in 1836, a friend of Charles Dickens named Captain Marryat allegedly fired a pistol at a shadowy figure standing in the doorway. In 1891, Marryat's daughter Florence offered a chilling description of her father's encounter with the Brown Lady: 'I have heard him describe how he watched her approaching nearer and nearer, through the chink of the door … the figure halted of its own accord before the door behind which he stood, and holding the lighted lamp she carried to her features, grinned in a malicious and diabolical manner at him.' Marryat – 'anything but lamb-like in disposition' – proceeded to discharge the revolver 'right in her face', at which point the apparition disappeared. Florence also shared that the pistol was given to her father by two men to protect himself from the lady, and those two men had also witnessed her before he fired and she vanished. Sightings continued sporadically over the years, with owners and visitors reporting visions of a lady on the staircase and the stairs could be seen through her.

It is important to remember that at the time the famous Brown Lady spirit photograph was published in December 1936, spiritualism had emerged as a trend. And a year or so before this photograph was taken, the Dowager Duchess Townshend, who was the incumbent lady of the house at the time and a 'staunch believer' in the supernatural, actually published a book of thirty-two 'true' ghost stories. She stated plainly that she believed Raynham Hall was haunted, and the Brown Lady of Raynham Hall story was the first entry in her book. As fascinating as her collection of ghost stories is, it does beg the question whether the Brown Lady legend and the spirit photograph of her gliding down and revealing the grandeur of the staircase was a publicity stunt to engage interest in Raynham Hall and reverse its declining income, or whether it was in fact the story of a true haunting.

14. WINCHESTER MYSTERY HOUSE

The origins of the haunting of Winchester mansion in California date back to the story of Sarah Pardee Winchester and the death of her baby daughter Annie in 1866, followed by her exceedingly wealthy husband, William Wirt, dying in 1881. The shattering double tragedy broke Sarah's heart and mind and she eventually became a recluse, bordering on insane.

In her despair, Sarah allegedly reached out to a Boston-based spiritualist medium called Adam Coons, although no historical records of Coons can be found. According to legend, Coons told her there was a curse on her entire family due to the many deaths caused by the repeating rifle the Winchester family had invented. The medium told Sarah she needed to make amends, and the only way to save her own life was to build a house for the ghosts of those killed by the weapon.

Sarah promptly sold her home in New Haven, Connecticut, and moved to California. She arrived in Santa Clara Valley in 1884, believing the spirit of her dead husband was guiding her. She soon found a six-bedroom mansion with acres of surrounding land that was being constructed, and she convinced the current owner to sell it to her. Sarah hired dozens of local workers, and every day for the next thirty-six years the house was deconstructed and reassembled, with rooms repeatedly demolished and rebuilt.

By 1906, the mansion had expanded to seven floors with numerous rooms, complete with elevators, towers, trap doors, skylights and other surprises. Sarah's highly creative but chaotic plans were a constant work in progress. She was obsessed by the number thirteen, with the walls containing thirteen panels, windows containing thirteen panes, some rooms having thirteen windows and so on. Every staircase but one had thirteen steps. The one exception surprised in another way, in that although it had forty-two steps, each step was two inches high. The 1906 San Francisco earthquake caused considerable damage but, undaunted, Sarah continued further expansion after the damage was repaired. In total it is thought that the house has 10,000 windows, 2,000 doors, forty-seven fireplaces, forty staircases, thirteen bathrooms and nine kitchens.

Rooms are still being discovered in the mystery house, with the Blue Room, a dedicated seance room, only being opened as recently as 2016. It is believed it was boarded up following the 1906 earthquake, when Sarah was trapped there and blamed evil spirits for causing the event. The room had no windows and just one door, and it was Sarah's private room, where she would go to meditate, connect with her departed husband and dream up plans for the house. There was a bizarre method in her madness: she wanted to ensure innocent spirits felt at home in the house but that the vengeful spirits of those killed by Winchester rifles would be so confused by its baffling maze-like design that they would not be able to cause any harm. This may explain the chimneys that were built but never used, as it was thought ghosts could enter through chimneys. Only two mirrors were put up, as Sarah believed ghosts were afraid of their own reflection. Every midnight hour, Sarah would walk the hallways in an erratic course to ensure any ghost following her and her spirit guides would be disorientated by the confusion of her course.

Reports of ghosts and paranormal activity began almost as soon as Sarah moved into the house. At midnight and 2 a.m. every night a bell would chime from the house; according to spirit lore, this is the arrival and departure time of spirits. Visitors to the house have reported eerie banging sounds, footsteps, voices and unusual smells. Staff members have even reported the full-blown apparition of Sarah herself. One guidebook warns that visitors may feel extreme temperature drops and experience a sense of presence, as well as flashes of light with no apparent source. One worker said he switched off all the lights in the house on closing up for the night, but when he got back to his car and looked at the house, he could see all the lights on the third floor had mysteriously been turned on again. Security guards have noted cold spots, doorknobs turning by themselves and security alarms triggering for no reason.

A couple of authors who spent the night alone in the house in 1979 reported that they heard the sound of a piano playing. They were not aware that when she was alive, Sarah was a keen piano player, and when she could not sleep, she would play the piano late into the night.

15. THE TOWER OF LONDON

Located on the north bank of the River Thames in the city of London, the Tower of London's history dates back to as early as 1066, the era of William the Conqueror, when it was a status-building secure fortress. Over the centuries it has been used as a royal palace and a zoo, but it is best known for its use as an unforgiving prison, with executions taking place within its walls and on Tower Hill. Many ghosts are associated with the Tower, but some of the most notorious include Edward V and his brother Richard – the two young princes who, in 1483, were imprisoned in the Tower and never seen again. Their ghosts are said to haunt the White Tower, with reports of disembodied laughter and crying and the apparition of two sad-looking little boys dressed in white and holding hands.

Anne Boleyn – the second wife of King Henry VIII who was beheaded in 1536 – is another famous Tower ghost. Her body was buried in the Chapel of St Peter ad Vincula, and some 340 years after her death, a soldier investigating a light burning in the empty chapel looked in a window to see a procession of historic knights and ladies led by the unfortunate queen. Her headless spectre is also said to pace the grounds, to the terror of those who encounter her.

Lady Jane Grey is also believed to haunt the Tower chapel. She was queen for just nine days before being imprisoned in the Tower and was eventually executed by Queen Elizabeth I for treason. Lady Jane's husband, Lord Guildford Dudley, was also executed, and it is said he haunts the cell in Beauchamp Tower, where the word 'Jane' is carved into the walls, allegedly by Dudley's ghostly hands.

In addition to royal ghosts, Guy Fawkes, who was imprisoned and tortured in the Tower in 1605 after his attempt to blow up the Houses of Parliament, is said to be heard screaming.

The botched execution of Margaret Pole, Countess of Salisbury, on Tower Green in 1541 for the crime of being the mother of Cardinal Pole, who opposed Henry's position as supreme leader of the Church, has given rise to reports of 'anguished disembodied screams'.

The Queen's House is believed to be haunted by the ghost of Elizabeth I's third cousin, Lady Arbella Stuart. She was imprisoned by James I for daring to marry the nephew of Lady Jane Grey, William Seymour, without royal permission. Arbella died of starvation in her prison, and her restless spirit stalks the Tower to this day.

On top of all that, a Welsh guardsman who was on duty at the Salt Tower in 1957 reported the apparition of the face of a young woman, and there have also been reports of a 'white figure' as well as the sounds of a disembodied sandal-wearing monk pacing the flagstones.

There's no doubt that due to the tragic events that have transpired there and the dark history trapped within its walls, if any place was going to be haunted, it would be the Tower. However, given the Tower is now such a famous tourist attraction, it is important to remember that 'terror sells'. And spare a thought for the Tower's most notorious residents – its ravens. Since the Norman Conquest they have roosted there, and legend has it that if the birds ever leave, it will signal the end of the monarchy. From 1946 onwards a flock of at least six ravens have been routinely installed, with their wings clipped to ensure they can never leave. In early 2021, Merlina, one of those ravens, went missing, prompting the Tower to release a statement reassuring a nervous public that there were still seven ravens – 'one more than the required six' – resident in the Tower.

16. THE TAJ MAHAL PALACE HOTEL

India boasts a number of allegedly haunted hotels open to the public, including Morgan House Tourist Lodge in Kalimpong and the Hotel Brij Raj Bhavan in Kota. But the Taj Mahal Palace in Mumbai has one of the most visceral backstories. It is believed to be lovingly haunted by one of the original architects who designed it.

First opened in 1903, the magnificently beautiful Taj Mahal

Palace stands imposingly opposite the Gateway of India, overlooking the Arabian Sea. Synonymous with style, luxury and majesty, it became a favourite place for celebrities, royalty and VIPs to visit – but it has also been no stranger to death and violence over the years, serving as a military hospital during the Second World War, as well as being subject to a horrific terrorist attack in 2008.

W. A. Chambers was one of the masterminds behind the opulent design of the Taj Mahal. The story goes that he drafted and carefully approved the blueprints for the construction before going on an overseas trip. However, on his return he found, to his utter shock and dismay, that his intricate blueprints had not been followed correctly. Indeed, there was a colossal mistake. The hotel was facing in the opposite direction to that which he intended.

Being a perfectionist, Chambers simply couldn't deal with the error caused by the oversight, especially as construction was in such an advanced stage it could not be reversed. Rather than face the humiliation, he took his own life and jumped to his death from the fifth floor of the building.

It is believed that the ghost of Chambers still wanders the halls of the hotel. Staff and guests have reported seeing in the corners of their eyes his forlorn and anxious ghost. The good news is that he is totally harmless, and even though strange noises and sighs and even his apparition have been spotted, these experiences do not typically incite feelings of dread among those who witness them. Quite the opposite, in fact – the feeling is that in death, just as in life, Chambers remains true to his perfectionist spirit. His only desire seems to be to silently observe, which is thought to contribute to staff standards remaining exceptionally high.

17. THE WASHOE CLUB

In the mid-1870s, Virginia City enjoyed a boom time, and skilled miners, gunslingers and entrepreneurs, and famous prostitutes, flocked to Comstock Lode hoping to strike gold. Opened on 1 June 1875, the Washoe Club is a towering brick building right in the heart of the city. It was the brainchild of mining millionaires, artists and writers who wanted a luxurious members-only meeting place in the area. Among other extravagances, it included a lavish parlour with Italian-made marble and bronze statues, an opulent billiard room and, of course, a richly overstocked wine room.

The best-laid plans for the club were derailed in 1875 by the great Virginia City Fire, which not only destroyed the booming club but much of Virginia City too. Members stopped paying their fees and the club struggled, though it still managed to reopen six months later in even more lavish style. This time it included a vast reception hall, a reading room in the shape of a grand piano, and more elegant cigar, billiard and wine rooms.

The timing of the ambitious reopening was once again not on the members' side, however. In 1881, due to mine fires and declining demand for their products, many members had to drastically curb their expenses and resign from the club. With its wealthy members disappearing fast, there was little that could be done to keep the club afloat, and by September 1897 it had closed down.

The old Washoe Club building was preserved and remains to this day. Over the years there have been numerous reports of paranormal activity, such as strange noises, voices, footsteps and full-blown apparitions. The frequency of these reports has given rise to paranormal investigations, seances and overnight lock-ins, some of which have been filmed for popular American ghost-hunting TV shows.

A young girl was allegedly killed in the basement and is believed to haunt the place, but the most well-known resident ghost is called Lena. It is said that in its opulent heyday, the upper floor of the club was once a brothel. A blonde prostitute was murdered on the third floor and her killer took his own life shortly afterwards. Several witnesses have spotted the apparition of a blonde woman repeatedly walking up the spiral staircase to the men's club and vanishing when she reaches the top. There is no way of knowing the name of the ghostly prostitute, but given the repeated sightings of her, club patrons decided she deserved one: Lena.

There is now an on-site Washoe Club Haunted Museum, lending further credibility to its reputation as the most spooky saloon in the west.

18. 50 BERKELEY SQUARE

Once believed to be the most haunted house in London, 50 Berkeley Square is an elegant Mayfair home. The building has been much researched ever since stories of alleged paranormal activity began circulating towards the end of the nineteenth century.

There are conflicting stories, but most are born of the fact that from 1859 to early 1874, the house was occupied by a deeply eccentric man called William Myers, a recluse who slept during the day and stayed awake at night, making strange sounds and stumbling about by candlelight. He lived in the house, slowly declining in mental health as each year passed until he died at the age of seventy-six.

During Myers' occupancy the house was seriously neglected, and that was when stories of hauntings began to circulate. There were so many stories that over time the house became known as 'Bloody Bones'. These stories included the ghost of a young girl who allegedly took her own life following sexual abuse. She was said to have thrown herself off the roof, but her ghost remained to haunt the attic and scare the life out of people staying in the house. She would appear as a lady in white or as a muddy mist driving those who saw it insane or making them run for their lives. Other stories replace the young girl with a man who was imprisoned in the attic and fed through a tiny hole in the door until he died. Another grisly rumour attributed the haunting in the attic to the ghost of a child who was killed by a deeply disturbed servant.

The house's reputation for being haunted further intensified in 1872. Myers was summoned by the local council for not paying his taxes; he was never prosecuted, allegedly because of fears he was possessed and his home haunted. In 1879, *Mayfair* magazine added fuel to the ghostly fire by reporting the story of a maidservant who lived in the house after Myers died and went mad after staying too long in the attic. She claimed something evil appeared in front of her with 'hideously glaring eyes'. A day after her sighting of the apparition, she was sent to an asylum, where she died. However, *Mayfair* commented that readers should not hastily jump to conclusions, because 'women may go mad now and again, without any ghostly dealings'.

A nobleman who stayed overnight in the attic room to prove it wasn't haunted may have proved the opposite. He promised to ring the bell if he needed assistance and the bell rang frantically. The owners rushed to his assistance but found him rigid with fear and without the power of speech.

In 1887, two sailors from HMS *Penelope* stayed in the attic. One claimed he saw the ghost of Myers in the night and the other was found dead outside, having fatally tripped in his haste to escape the horror within 50 Berkeley Square.

Although there have been no reported deaths or descents into insanity associated with the attic or anywhere else in the house since the 1930s, there have been continued reports by visitors of strange noises coming from within, and modern ghost hunters report disembodied voices and feelings of intense dread.

Sceptics robustly dismiss rumours of ghostly activity at 50 Berkeley Square as the product of nonsense, speculation and exaggeration of the natural noises old houses make. Others believe the house remains a paranormal magnet, and just touching the exterior brickwork can send a chill down the spine of those with a sensitive disposition.

19. THE TRANS-ALLEGHENY LUNATIC ASYLUM

Western State Hospital, also known as the Trans-Allegheny Lunatic Asylum, is a vast building that stands beside the West Fork River in Staunton, Virginia. It was originally created with the noble intention of being a peaceful sanctuary for those who suffered from mental illness. It ended up being exactly the opposite and swiftly earned a reputation for hopelessness and terror.

The hospital was designed to care for 250 patients, but due to overcrowding, the number of patients admitted had reached over 700 by 1880 and it became a breeding ground for poor patient care, death – and ghosts.

The hospital's name was changed to Western State Hospital in 1913 due to people's increasing discomfort with using the words 'lunatic' and 'asylum'. Despite this, straitjackets and other violent and 'crazy' experimental methods, such as fever therapy, ice baths and insulin shocks, were routinely used to contain patients, including the hideous 'lobotomy'.

From the 1950s onwards the overcrowding increased even further, with the hospital holding more than 2,500 patients. Many were wrongfully admitted. As late as the 1980s, dubious treatment methods continued with patients locked in cages. Mercifully the experimental nature of the 'hospital' was shut down completely in the 1990s.

The combination of mental illness, violence and torture that took place at Western State (it was also the site of much bloody conflict during the American Civil War) has given rise to many reports of alleged paranormal activity. Visitors to the ruined site of the hospital claim to have encountered ghosts and spirits, including in the asylum graveyard, which is believed to be haunted, with over 3,000 unnamed bodies buried there. Muffled screams from the graves and shadowy figures have been reported over the years.

Within the hospital walls, to this day staff and visitors report the sound of dragging feet along the hallways, as well as unexplained noises and feeling a sudden chill which disappears when mysterious footsteps have passed by.

Wards C and F on the third floor once used to contain the most disturbed men and women, and visitors to both wards have reported hearing disembodied whispers, delirious laughter and screams. It is the fourth floor, however, that is believed to be the most paranormally active, with reports of doors opening and closing by themselves as well as sounds of banging without any explainable cause and the echoes of blood-curdling screams.

There is also said to be the ghost of a nurse lingering in the hospital. The story goes that she was murdered and her body was not discovered until two months later, under a stairwell. There have also been reports of the apparitions of wounded men, perhaps dating back to the hospital's Civil War history.

Then there is the haunting ghost story of little 'Lilly'. Visitors have reported spotting a young girl wearing Victorian clothes. She is said to look around three years old and gives the impression of simply wanting to play in the hospital hallways. She often runs to a staircase and then vanishes. There is no telling who she is, and her name was given to her after repeated reports of her presence there. She may have been the daughter of a patient who gave birth while locked in solitary confinement, the child then taken away to an orphanage, where she probably died, her restless spirit continuing to roam the abandoned hospital, which is now a popular paranormal tourist attraction, all these years later.

20. OTTAWA JAIL

Before its closure in 1972, Ottawa Jail in Canada was an infamous, sinister prison. It was built in the early 1860s and many of the cells had holes in the walls instead of windows, which meant the wellbeing of the inmates was dictated by the seasons.

In the 1950s, when the courtyard was being dug up to facilitate the building of a bridge, 140 bodies of executed prisoners were discovered. Perhaps more alarming is that only a portion of the courtyard was dug up, so there is no telling how many more bodies lie beneath the heavy concrete.

Today, Ottawa Jail has reopened as a youth hostel and those visiting can request an overnight stay in one of those unforgiving cells. They can also tour death row, the original gallows used for public hangings now placed deep in the basement, and isolation cells with rings on the walls used to handcuff prisoners face down on the ground. Visitors can also inspect the nameless graves of prisoners who died during their incarceration. Not surprisingly, given Ottawa hostel's harsh past, paranormal encounters have been reported ever since the hostel opened.

Overnight guests have reported Bible-reading shadowy figures at the feet of their beds when they wake in the night. Others say they have witnessed apparitions of former inmates in their cells or on death row. One particular guest heard an eerie humming sound as he tried to sleep, though he described it as an 'amazing' experience.

One of the most well-known prisoners at Ottawa Jail was Patrick James Whelan, who allegedly murdered diplomat Thomas D'Arcy McGee. Patrick was imprisoned there before his execution and continued to assert his innocence throughout his trial, appealing his sentence to the very last, but to no avail. He was hanged on 11 February 1869 before a crowd of some 5,000 people. His body was supposed to be buried in Montreal, but he was buried in the prison grounds instead. It is thought his forlorn ghost has never stopped pacing backwards and forwards, forever protesting his innocence in his death row cell.

21. A GHOSTLY HITCHHIKER

There is a lengthy and deserted stretch of road from Adelaide to the Yorke Peninsula in Port Wakefield, South Australia, which, if various accounts from drivers on that road are to be believed, may have a resident ghostly hitchhiker.

Reports began in the 1940s and have recurred sporadically ever since. Typically, it is a stormy and dark night and people are driving along Port Wakefield Road. One account came from a young couple who said they picked up a man wearing his air force uniform. He was hitching a ride and asked if he could be taken to an address in Adelaide. The couple agreed, and the hitchhiker sat silently in the back seat of the car. When they turned around in the car to say goodbye on arrival at the destination, he was no longer there. He had vanished.

Seeking answers and wondering whether they had imagined things, the couple knocked on the door of the house. A woman answered and broke down in tears. She told them that her son had died during the Second World War. He had been in the air force and his flight had taken off from Mallala, which was close by. The authorities told her that they believed her son's body had been buried in an unknown location. She told the couple the hitchhiker must have been her son's spirit trying to find his way home.

Another story came from a local businessman who picked up a man wearing air force uniform. When he stopped to use the restroom at a service station, the man came with him. As they both went inside, the hitchhiker vanished.

Reports of ghostly hitchhikers always seem to capture public and media imagination as well as the attention of many curious paranormal investigators. They have become the inspiration for bestselling books and horror movies. But perhaps the real sadness is that there is often the element of a tragic death or the murder of an innocent or vulnerable person involved in the backstory, leaving the ghost of the victim and those who loved them unable to find peace.

22. CHILLING CASTLES

Britain's haunted castles truly are a ghost hunter's dream. An entire paranormal guidebook could be written about each one of them. And that is exactly what Lady Leonora, Countess of Tankerville, owner of thirteenth-century Chillingham Castle in Northumberland, England, did. From 1895 onwards, she started to write down her paranormal experiences at Chillingham, which apparently began with a vision in a dream before she had even moved in. When she finally visited the place, she stated, 'This is the second time I find myself approaching the gates of Chillingham Castle but strangely it is the first time I have actually been here.' By 1925, she had enough experiences to complete her book, *The Ghosts of Chillingham Castle*, where she confidently asserted, 'I had no idea there could be so many apparitions living under one roof.' These included the ghost of a child whose cries can be heard on the stroke of midnight. Known as the Radiant Boy, once his cries have faded away, those who have stayed in the castle report seeing a bright halo of light as a young boy dressed in blue approaches them. The rustle of an elderly woman's dress and the inexplicable scent of rosewater can also be sensed.

Today, the castle keeps the spirit of Lady Leonora's ghost-hunting diary alive and offers ghosts tours, marketing the castle as 'the most haunted castle in England'. But Windsor Castle emerges as a strong contender for that title with the sheer number of royal ghosts spotted there over the years. These include King Henry VIII dragging his swollen, ulcerated leg in the courtyard, as well as Queen Elizabeth I, King Charles I and King George III, who put in cameo appearances in the royal library.

Of course, haunted castles aren't restricted to England. Staking a claim for most haunted castle in Scotland is Glamis Castle. In the early 1820s, the first son of the 11th Earl of Strathmore was born deformed with no neck, tiny limbs and an egg-like body. The baby was not expected to live and was locked away in a secret room, but to everyone's astonishment he lived a long life, with some accounts suggesting he lived to the ripe old age of 100. Over the years there have been sightings of the 'monster of Glamis' and strange shadows on part of the battlements known as 'The Mad Earl's Walk'. Gwydir Castle in Wales is believed to be haunted by the ghost of a murdered servant girl whose body was buried in the walls, her spirit accompanied forevermore by the foul smell of putrefaction, and Leap Castle in the Republic of Ireland abounds with reports of ghosts. Built in the fourteenth century, it witnessed much inter-clan bloodshed, including a red wedding massacre at a family reunion in a banqueting hall. Brother slaying brother also took place within the chapel, earning it the title 'the Bloody Chapel'. In 1922, a secret room was discovered packed with the unnamed remains of Leap Castle victims. Locals report that from time to time the windows of the Bloody Chapel inexplicably light up late into the night.

23. HAUNTED CEMETERIES

Cemeteries are often dark, sombre, quiet places where you unconsciously lower your head and hold your breath – so they're the perfect setting for a haunting and breathing in the energy of the spirits that lie there. Arguably any cemetery, wherever it is located around the world and whoever may be buried there, is haunted by memories and untold stories. But there are some American cemeteries which seem to attract more reports of paranormal activity than others, perhaps because some are also tourist attractions with more visitors than less well-known cemeteries.

Leading the haunted way is the Old Western burial ground in Maryland. Locals believe that ghosts linger there whenever the sun sets. The cemetery was built by the first Presbyterian church of Baltimore in 1787. It's possible much of its haunted reputation is related to the fact that it is the final resting place of several famous generals and none other than paranormal author and poet Edgar Allan Poe. There have been numerous sightings of Poe, wearing a long black coat, a wide-brimmed hat and a scarf covering his face, standing sadly in front of his grave. Also, part of the graveyard can only be entered by way of catacombs – dark tunnels below the church where many ghosts are said to make their home.

A similar paranormal reputation applies to St Louis Cemetery No. 1 in Louisiana. This cemetery dates back to 1789 and is the final resting place for the noted voodoo queen Marie Laveau, who has been seen wearing her trademark red and white turban, meandering among the graves. Close behind in terms of reports of hauntings is Stull Cemetery in Kansas. There have been numerous reported sightings and encounters with ghosts there, perhaps ignited by the belief that the cemetery is one of the seven portals to hell. This story began in 1974, when a paper published in the University of Kansas student newspaper boldly stated that Satan himself visited the cemetery at least twice a year. Debate continues as to whether this was a 'fraternity prank' or not.

Bachelor's Grove abandoned cemetery in Chicago, Illinois, commands attention for its reported sightings of dancing ghosts as well as unexplained orbs of light. There have been reports of the ghost of a farmer and his horse who died when they were dragged to their deaths in a nearby pond, as well as a 1940s gangster-style car that appears on the road and then vanishes. The *Chicago Sun-Times* published a photograph of what became known as the 'Madonna of Bachelor's Grove'. If you search for the photo online, you will find a woman wearing old-fashioned attire sitting on a gravestone. According to the photographer the woman was not visible when the photo was taken. Some believe this may be the 'white lady', the ghost of a mother buried next to her young child, who has been seen walking the graveyard at night with her baby in her arms.

The Resurrection Cemetery in Chicago also boasts a resident spirit: Resurrection Mary. The story goes that in the 1930s, this vivacious and beautiful girl went to a local dance wearing a floating white dress and dancing shoes but was killed by a hit-and-run driver while she was walking. Her family buried her in Resurrection Cemetery in her dancing dress and shoes, and there have been dozens of reports of motorists picking up this well-dressed hitchhiker and chatting with her before she vanishes into thin air outside the cemetery.

24. BORLEY RECTORY

Once dubbed 'the most haunted house in England', Borley Rectory in the county of Essex was intensively investigated between 1929 and 1938 by famous ghost hunter and founder of the National Laboratory of Psychical Research in London, Harry Price.

The rectory, a gloomy red building, was originally built in 1863 by the Reverend Henry Dawson Ellis Bull to house his big family of fourteen children. It all began when Ethel, one of the reverend's daughters, said she saw a ghost that looked like a nun in dark robes on the afternoon of 28 July 1900.

Local legend held that the house was built on the site of a thirteenth-century monastery where a nun and monk fell in love but were murdered before eloping together. The nun and a man wearing a tall dark hat have been spotted several times after that first sighting by Ethel and her sisters. Ethel maintained her story throughout her long life. She died in 1963 at the age of ninety-three, saying, 'What would be the use of an old lady like me waiting to meet her maker telling a lot of fairy stories?'

When Price started his investigation in 1929, the residents – Reverend G. E. Smith and his wife, who were both paranormal sceptics – told him that as soon as they had moved in, they had experienced shadowy figures, unexplained noises and whispers, phantom footsteps and mysterious smoke and smells, as well as doors banging, writing appearing on the wall and doorbells ringing when nobody was there, to name but a few things. Seances were also held, with rapping responses to questions and even alleged appearances by the ghostly nun. Price said he experienced the phenomenon himself, and in his book *The Most Haunted House in England*, which was published in 1940, he claimed that Borley was the 'best authenticated case in the annals of psychical research'.

In 1929, the Smiths moved out and the Reverend Forster and

his wife moved in. With no decrease in terrifying paranormal incidents occurring for the new residents, Price moved back in to investigate some more. The Forsters left Borley in 1935, and Price leased the property himself for a year. During this year he witnessed further paranormal activity and began writing his book, where he recorded in great detail his use of camera equipment and other methods of reporting ghostly activity.

At one point, Price had forty assistants helping him research Borley. Many of those assistants were psychics and mediums. Some dropped out because they could detect nothing, but others proposed that the monk and nun had been strangled and were buried in the garden at the residence, longing for a proper burial and mass.

Price left in 1938, convinced that Borley was built on the site of a medieval monastery even though there was no documented proof and the only records to be found stated that it had once been the site of a church. His book about Borley received a great critical reception from psychical researchers but was also heavily criticized for being overblown. In 1939, the house was burned to the ground by an oil lamp being accidentally knocked over. It was left in ruins until 1944, when it was demolished.

After Price died in 1948, his research file was reopened by psychical researchers Trevor Hall, Eric Dingwell and Kathleen Goldney. Reporter Charles Sutton asserted that Price had faked much of the evidence. He had visited the rectory once with Price and been hit by a random pebble. Later, he discovered that Price carried pebbles in his pockets.

Mrs Mabel Smith, a previous resident of the rectory, signed a document in 1949 saying the phenomena was likely 'normally produced' during her time in the house. She suspected that Price had fabricated evidence, and this theory was backed by Dingwell, Hall and Goldney when they published their own book about Borley. They proposed that everything that had happened could be explained by Price fabricating stories to boost his writing career. They also said that Borley Rectory was the perfect residence because its gloomy design lent itself to the power of suggestion.

The rectory was an old, Gothic place, and Price may have been susceptible to bending the truth and/or deeply sensitive to atmospheres. But this might not explain away the multiple reported incidents by numerous unrelated people over the many years Borley was the subject of paranormal debate.

And surely Ethel, the little girl behind the first reported ghostly encounter, would have found it cathartic and important to reveal the truth before her death? Perhaps the truth went with Ethel to her grave and with the rectory when it was demolished. But all the paranormal reports, the investigation by Price and other leading psychical researchers, and the inevitable TV shows and movies they inspired have confirmed its status as allegedly one of the most haunted houses in Britain and maybe even the world.

25. THE CRESCENT HOTEL

In the isolated American town of Eureka Springs, Arkansas, on the ridge of West Mountain, there lies the Grand Old Lady of the Ozarks, also known as the Crescent Hotel. This Gothic-looking hotel is alive with ghosts, if reports are to believed.

Built in 1886, the hotel was ambitiously designed with thick granite walls. It initially attracted people from all over America who wanted to take advantage of Eureka Springs for its 'healing waters'. It was thought that the water could cure ailments and being drenched in it was restorative. The water was bottled and shipped out for those who could not make it to the hotel. The local railroad and town benefited greatly from health tourists and the shipping of the bottled water.

Enthusiasm for and belief in the power of the 'healing waters' declined around the turn of the century, and this impacted not just the hotel but the entire town. In 1908, the hotel was transformed into Crescent College and Conservatory for young women. During the summer holidays the hotel reopened, but both school and hotel could not sustain enough funds to remain open, and by 1930, both had closed down.

After that the hotel changed hands several times. By far the most notorious owner was Dr Norman Baker, a radio presenter who claimed he could cure cancer and styled himself as a doctor even though he had no formal qualifications. He bought Eureka Springs after encountering legal problems when he opened his first cancer hospital in Iowa. Baker bought the hotel in July 1937, spent a lot of money from unknown sources on repurposing it as a hospital and then installed himself, his medical crew and some 144 patients there.

The Crescent Hospital stated that it did not need to take X-rays or use surgery or even medication to save lives, as the only cure needed was Eureka spring water. Many of Baker's patients died there, and although there is no proof to verify this, legend has it that during a renovation human skeletons were discovered inside the walls. Those skeletons were said to be patients Baker had experimented on. In 1940, he was arrested for making false medical claims and went to prison for four years in Leavenworth, and his hospital was shut down permanently.

The first reports of alleged hauntings at the Crescent came in 1946, when new owners restored and reopened the hotel. Staff members started to experience uncanny things in the rooms and in the hallways. A telephone switchboard even had to be removed because of repeated phone calls coming in from a basement recreation room that was unused and locked, so no one could get in. The key to the room was kept at the front desk and there was only one way to enter and exit the room. On one occasion when a staff member went to check inside the room when a call came in, the telephone was off the hook. On returning upstairs, the staff member heard the recreation room call again. And ghostly encounters weren't just reported by staff. Hotel guests reported waking in the night to shadowy figures standing at the end of their bed. Apparitions in the lobby dressed in Victorian clothes have been seen before vanishing, and a ghostly nurse pushes a trolley down a hallway.

There have even been reports of Baker standing close to a staircase. Housekeepers have also reported meeting a ghostly lady called Theodora in Room 419. She tells people she is a cancer patient and then disappears. Another focus of paranormal investigation is Room 218, where one of the original Irish stonemasons working on the hotel's construction in 1886 apparently plunged to his death from the window.

The Crescent Hotel continues to attract the interest of paranormal investigators and has the reputation of being one of the most haunted hotels in America. There are so many ghostly stories associated with the place that haunted tours happen there all year round.

26. THE WEEPING WOMAN OF MEXICO

In Mexican folklore, the Weeping Woman (also known as *La Llorona*, Spanish for 'weeper') is said to be a wailing ghostly woman who floats around the canals and riverbanks in the borough of Xochimilco in Mexico City at night, although she is also said to appear in other versions and locations, including the United States, Guatemala and Venezuela.

As is often the case with legends, there are variations on the story. In one version, *La Llorona* killed her own child and wanders the earth in eternal torment. In another, she is looking for her murdered children. In another, she had children but fell head over heels in love with a man who didn't want them, so in an attempt to keep him, she drowned her own children. Overcome with grief and guilt, she then drowned herself. And then there is the story that she was a lady called Maria who found out her husband was having an affair and murdered her children as an act of revenge. Whatever version of the story, there is a haunting theme of a weeping woman torn apart by grief and guilt while searching in vain for her children.

La Llorona is described as shapely and soaking wet. She is dressed entirely in white or black. Her hair is flowing and her nails are long and shaped like daggers, but she has no face. As well as the canals where she is typically seen, she is also believed to haunt deserted places, where she likes to entice and even kill drunken men who stumble upon her. Sometimes she appears on the roadside to hitch a ride and when she enters the car, she vanishes. Whatever the scenario, any sighting of her is believed to bring bad luck or death within a year.

There is a possibility that the story has a historical basis. Around 1550, an Indian princess fell in love with an Italian nobleman and they had twins. Although the nobleman promised to marry the princess, he married someone else instead. In a fit of rage and heartbreak, the princess murdered the twins with a dagger. Driven mad by her terrible deed, she then wandered the streets in torn and bloody clothes wailing for her children. The authorities arrested and executed her, and from then on it was said her ghost was cursed to wander the streets for eternity. Folklore experts suggest another origin for this story that may date back to ancient Aztec mythology. The goddess Cihuacōātl is depicted dressed in white and carrying an empty cradle, and it is said she perpetually cries for her lost child.

It is credible that the story of *La Llorona* was originally told to children to ensure they came home safely before darkness fell, and also perhaps to warn husbands and lovers that hell hath no fury like a woman scorned.

27. THE STANLEY HOTEL

Built in 1909 by Freelan Oscar Stanley, a Massachusetts entrepreneur and inventor, the Stanley Hotel in Estes Park, Colorado, become world-famous when it was used as the setting for Stanley Kubrick's iconic movie *The Shining*. Prior to the movie, the Stanley Hotel was the inspiration for Stephen King's original novel of the same name. The story goes that King stayed at the hotel with his wife during a snowstorm. It was an unforgettable experience for him.

F. O. Stanley lived at the Stanley Hotel with his wife, Flora, who was a talented pianist. Since her death in 1940, there have been reports of mysterious piano playing heard at night coming from the music room, but on inspection there is nobody there and her beloved Steinway piano is locked away.

Room 217, which plays a key role in both the movie and the book, is to this day believed to be haunted by the ghost of a chambermaid called Elizabeth Wilson, who died there. There are conflicting accounts, but the consensus seems to be that she was not murdered in the room but blasted out of the window by an accidental gas explosion in 1911. She walked into the room holding a lit candle, unaware that there was a gas leak in the room. Room 217 is the room where King and his wife spent the night, and a lucid nightmare that haunted King's sleep that night served as inspiration for the classic horror book.

Room 428 is also believed to have a resident ghost – that of a looming cowboy – and there have been sightings of Stanley himself in the billiards room, as well as shadowy figures on the staircase, a few of which have been captured on camera and can be viewed online. Unknown ghostly presences have been detected in the tunnels beneath the hotel, and many guests report feelings of dread on entering the hotel. Not to mention that both staff and guests have reported hearing whispers and the giggles of children as they walk down the corridors and incidents where lights have somehow switched on by themselves.

It is no surprise that the hotel makes the most of its haunted and sinister reputation, offering haunted hotel tours. *The Shining* plays on repeat on in-house TV channels, and for those with the courage to stay the night, it is possible to experience a night in Room 217. All this strongly suggests that it is the book and the movie that have curated the Stanley Hotel's haunted reputation, and the power of suggestion is strong. But then, if you visit the hotel and take a look at old photographs of Stanley hanging there, it can feel like a strangely unsettling warning. He looks out of sorts, as though he has just seen a ghost.

28. BLACKPOOL PLEASURE BEACH

Visited by hundreds of thousands of people each year, Blackpool Pleasure Beach in Lancashire, England, was founded by entrepreneur Alderman William George Bean and his partner John Outhwaite. In 1896, on returning from a failed attempt to strike rich as an advertising giant in the United States, Bean decided to seek investors to help him build and open two amusement parks.

The Pleasure Beach was officially opened in 1905 and was an ambitious, pioneering experiment offering never-before-seen attractions in the UK. The experiment worked. It remains a popular tourist attraction to this day – and along the way it has also gathered a reputation as one of the most haunted places to visit in the country.

Blackpool Pleasure Beach's ice rink has repeated reports of an invisible ice skater using the rink when it is closed to the public.

Staff have reported hearing the sound of skating when there is no one on the ice. Objects have reportedly moved of their own accord and windows inexplicably slammed shut. Staff there have also experienced feelings of heaviness and dread and of being watched when darkness falls. This feeling of being watched is not restricted to the ice rink – many staff members working at other Blackpool Pleasure venues have reported a presence too. There have been reports of a disembodied woman's voice singing and of pictures mysteriously falling off the walls, as well as lights turning on and off for no obvious reason.

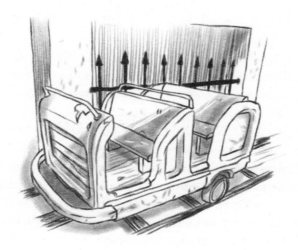

On top of the invisible signs, there have also been sightings of fully fledged apparitions. One of those appears to resemble Karl Marx, the well-known nineteenth-century German philosopher and activist. One visitor described seeing a ghost lingering at the Pleasure Beach bar in the early hours of the morning. The Sir Hiram Maxim gift shop allegedly boasts the resident ghost of a playful young girl, believed to be about eight or nine years old.

The most notorious ghost, however, is ironically one that is said to haunt the Pleasure Beach's ghost train. He is believed to be the ghost of a dedicated train operator who used to work there, and although it is not certain who this employee was, the ghostly presence has been given the name 'Cloggy' because both visitors and staff have reported hearing the eerie sound of clogs clicking around the attraction. It seems his dedication to ensuring the ghost train ran smoothly didn't end with his life.

29. BRIDGE TO THE OTHER SIDE

Whether they have a reputation for being haunted or not, bridges are a poetic metaphor for crossing over from this life to the afterlife.

One of the most famous haunted bridges is the Eunice Williams Covered Bridge in Greenfield, Massachusetts. The bridge was named after a woman called Eunice Williams, the wife of a local clergyman, who was killed in 1704. The story goes that she was taken captive by Native American and French forces at the English settlement at Deerfield. Dozens of people died in the attack, and survivors were forced to march hundreds of miles to New France, where their fate would be decided. A few days before the attack, Williams, a thirty-nine-year-old mother of five children, had just given birth to her sixth child. She collapsed with exhaustion while being marched along the Green River. She was killed by a tomahawk blow and her body was left to rot by the river as the gruelling march carried on. The covered bridge was built at the spot where she fell in around 1870 and is believed to be perpetually haunted by her presence.

According to legend, Eunice will appear on a moonless or dark night if you are crossing the bridge and honk your horn. Her exhausted apparition has also been spotted under the bridge and on the banks of the river. Sometimes she screams for help and her screams carry on throughout the night as if she is reliving her final days. Sometimes she has walked alongside people crossing the bridge and appears to mistake them for members of her family.

30. BORGVATTNET VICARAGE

Borgvattnet Vicarage in Jämtland, northern Sweden, dates back to 1876. At a glance it looks picturesque, humble and unassuming, and the village of Borgvattnet itself only has a few dozen residents. However, appearances can be deeply deceptive.

From 1927 onwards, vicars and their families living in the vicarage were all eager to leave as soon as they moved in, reporting numerous strange, scary experiences. Both residents and guests in the vicarage have claimed to have witnessed ghostly shadow figures in the corners of their eyes and have spoken of objects moving without any reason. Disembodied footsteps, musical notes with no source and the sound of invisible crying women have all been reported. One of the most eerie reports involved an old rocking chair, which likes to rock on its own as if something or someone unseen is sitting in it.

Even though paranormal activity was first noticed at the vicarage in the late 1920s, it was not until the last priest, Erik Lindgren, moved into the house in 1945 that it became well known that the home was haunted. During an Agricultural Society meeting in December 1947, a journalist who had heard rumours about the vicarage asked Erik about them. The priest was not ashamed to go public with his experiences and told the journalist about how he had heard unexplained footsteps, candles were constantly blown out and on more than one occasion he had actually bumped into an unseen presence.

There are a number of theories as to the reason for the vicarage's haunted reputation. One is that the first priest there had an affair with a young local girl. Some believe he raped her, but what is agreed is that when the girl became pregnant, the priest locked her in a small hut in the backyard and when she gave birth, the baby was killed and buried there. It is not clear whether the girl was also killed or if she killed her own baby. Other theories have been put forward, including former servants with grudges to bear and former priests watching over the residence.

In the early 1980s, a priest called Tore Forslund, also known as the 'ghost priest', came to the town when he heard the stories about the haunted vicarage. He promised he would rid the place of any ghosts, but the exorcism he performed clearly didn't work, because stories about disembodied screams, glimpses of shadowy people and objects inexplicably moving continued. He left the area a year later, his ghost priest reputation in tatters.

Today the vicarage has become a bed and breakfast, but it may only be suitable for those willing to sleep with one eye open. The proprietors have been known to reward guests with a certificate saying they made it through the night at Borgvattnet.

31. PENDLE HILL

Contenders for most haunted spots in the scenic British countryside include Prestbury in Cheltenham, Gloucestershire, where the ghost of the Black Abbot is believed to haunt the local church and high street, and Pluckley in Ashford, Kent, which boasts many resident ghosts as well as a forest area called the 'Screaming Woods' that allegedly echoes with disembodied screams. However, in recent years first place has perhaps gone to Pendle Hill in Lancashire.

Pendle Hill is also known as Penhul. It is a Bronze Age burial site; the location where George Fox, founder of the Quakers, had his first vision; and where Richard Towneley's barometer experiment of 1661 discovered that atmospheric pressure decreases significantly with altitude. However, it is its documented links to the Lancashire witch trials which have made it world-famous; to this day visitors climb the hill to feel its allegedly macabre energy.

The story of the Pendle Hill witches is clearly recorded and documented, and this makes it as fascinating for historians as it is for ghost hunters. In 1612, a family of local peasants who lived in Malkin Tower in the shadow of the hill were accused of witchcraft and being in league with the devil. The reports state they had supernatural powers and made clay effigies using human hair and the teeth of animals. There were a number of unexplained illnesses at the time which either killed the victim or left them in extreme pain. In addition, milk was immediately turning sour and the cattle were dying mysteriously.

Locals lived in fear of the family and were too afraid to go near the hill and confront them. However, eventually a local magistrate by the name of Roger Norwell found the courage to arrest two of them. They were put on trial, and a few days later the rest were also arrested for witchcraft. During the trial one of the accused died, ten were found guilty and executed by hanging, and one was found not guilty.

At the time of the Lancashire trials, thousands of others were executed for witchcraft, but the detailed records of the Pendle witches has ensured their stories have never died. Their ghosts are believed to haunt the buildings and the village still, and especially the hill itself, with visitors reporting inexplicable feelings of anger and fear when they visit the grounds. Locals fear visiting the hill when night falls due to repeated sightings of figures dancing around on the barren hillside.

In 2011, engineers working on a construction project were stunned to discover the ruins of a seventeenth-century cottage under a grass mount in the Lower Black Moss reservoir in a village in the shadow of the hill. It was a witch's cottage, complete with cat bones bricked into the walls. This remarkable find could well have been the infamous Malkin Tower of the Pendle witches.

32. THE WHITE HOUSE

The White House is arguably the most famous haunted house in the world. The mansion at 1600 Pennsylvania Avenue in Washington DC has been the residence and workplace of the President of the United States since 1800.

The land the White House was built on was given to the government in the 1870s by a man called David Burns. It is thought he haunts the Rose Room and the Yellow Oval Room, with some reporting hearing a mysterious voice announcing itself: 'I'm Mr Burns.' There's also believed to be an apparition of a black cat that haunts the house on the evening before national tragedies occur, like the assassination of President Kennedy. However, the most well-known resident ghosts at the White House are, not surprisingly, presidential ones.

Apparitions of both John Adams – the second president of the United States – and his wife, Abigail, have been seen floating through the halls lost in thought or, curiously enough, carrying wet clothes to dry in the East Room. Thomas Jefferson, the third president, has been heard playing the violin in the Yellow Oval Room. James Madison, the fourth president, and his wife Dolley are believed to haunt and be fiercely protective of the rose garden Dolley planted. Andrew Jackson, the seventh president, has also been heard, but this time observers report a deep-sounding laugh. Meanwhile, President William Henry Harrison, the ninth president and the first to pass away while he was still in office, is believed to haunt the attic, and the presence of the tenth president, John Tyler, lingers in the Blue Room.

Of all the presidential ghosts reported in the White House, it is Abraham Lincoln, the sixteenth president, that has become the most notorious – so much so that the phrase 'Lincoln's ghost' is much used. British prime minister Winston Churchill spent a night in the Lincoln Bedroom in 1940, and as he emerged from his bath still smoking his signature cigar, he allegedly encountered Lincoln's smiling ghost standing beside the fireplace, leaning against the mantelpiece. The account is remarkable in that the apparition was so realistic, Churchill attempted to engage in conversation with it, saying, 'Good evening, Mr President, you seem to have me at a disadvantage.' As soon as Churchill uttered this greeting, the apparition vanished.

In 1942, Queen Wilhelmina of the Netherlands was visiting the White House and reported seeing Lincoln's ghost, dressed in a top hat and tails, standing at the door of her bedroom. She fainted in shock. And over the years several other presidents, including Harry S. Truman and Theodore Roosevelt, as well as staffers and visitors, have caught glimpses of Lincoln's ghost or heard mysterious footsteps and knocks.

It is perhaps only fitting that of all the presidents, it is Lincoln's presence that lingers most heavily, because during his lifetime he seems to have been drawn to the mysterious. This includes a famous account of a precognitive dream he had that may have predicted his own death. According to this account on 14 April 1865, a few days before his assassination Lincoln shared with a small group of friends, which included his wife, Mary Todd, a striking dream he'd had. In this dream he entered the East Room of the White House and saw a corpse with a sheet covering it. Mourners surrounded the corpse and solders were guarding it. Lincoln asked one of the soldiers who had died and was informed in his dream that it was the president, who had been killed by an assassin.

Doubt has been cast on this account, as it did not appear until twenty years after Lincoln's death, but whether it is true or not, it does seem that Lincoln was fascinated by the precognitive potential of dreams. On the morning of his assassination, members of his cabinet recounted that he told them about a dream he'd had the night before of sailing at great speed across an unknown sea. He also revealed that this dream had happened to him before on previous occasions. Nearly always, it prefaced some great or important event happening a few days later.

33. MUSEUM OF ART, HO CHI MINH CITY

The corridors of the Museum of Art in Ho Chi Minh City in Vietnam are believed to be haunted by the ghost of a lonely and seriously unhappy young girl. Built in 1934, the museum was originally an office building and also the family home of a super-wealthy Chinese real estate magnate called Uncle Hua (Hua Bon Hoa) who owned thousands of properties in the city.

The property tycoon had a daughter, Hứa Tiêu Lan. She had many suitors, but when she was sixteen she suddenly disappeared entirely from the social scene after contracting leprosy. Her father was deeply superstitious and believed his daughter's leprosy was a curse, so he hid her illness from everyone and she was kept locked up entirely alone in her room. Nobody was allowed to interact with her except the maids, who were told not to talk to her or look at her disfigured, ulcer-ridden face. Over time she lost her hair, her eyelashes, her appetite and her will to live. She died a silent death.

Reports differ from this point, with some claiming that her

body was buried in a coffin in her room and others saying there was a fake funeral, as when the coffin was unearthed, it was empty. Another account suggests that Hua, unable to process his daughter's death, continued to ask the maids to leave food for her even though she was dead. Whatever truly happened, after her death rumours about her ghost immediately began to spread. Passers-by reported seeing a shadowy figure with a disfigured face in the windows or floating through the halls. Others heard what sounded like a young girl sobbing frantically.

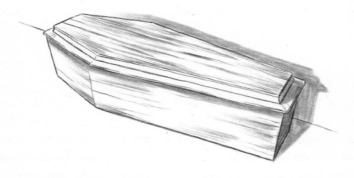

Since the building became a popular museum of fine arts, from the 1980s onwards there have been sightings by museum staff and visitors of her forlorn apparition and also of disembodied sobbing. Some have reported seeing the shadowy figure of a young girl in the corner of their eye, but when they turn to look at her, there is nobody there.

In 1973, the story was turned into a blockbuster movie called *The Ghost of the Hua Family*, and ghost hunters continue to try to discover the truth of what exactly happened to this young girl whose body has never been found. At no point has the Hua family addressed or verified any aspect of this story, including – as there are records for his sons but none can be discovered for a daughter – whether Hua's daughter ever existed at all.

34. GETTYSBURG

The most decisive and deadliest battle of the American Civil War was fought at Gettysburg, Pennsylvania, between 1 and 3 July 1863. Today the battlefield attracts millions of tourists every year, and many have reported feeling a sense of dread and fear when they are there, with some even reporting that they have actually heard and/or seen images from the battle.

In the town of Gettysburg and on the battlefield itself, disembodied screams have been heard, as well as gunfire and apparitions of the wounded. After the battle, bodies were strewn everywhere in the formation of rocks known as the Devil's Den, and there have been numerous sightings there of apparitions of wounded soldiers. According to one tour guide, a group of tourists witnessed what they believed to be a historical re-enactment at the summit of Little Round Top, a strategic hill secured by Union forces during the battle and the scene of relentless bloodshed. Later, they were astonished to discover that no such re-enactment had taken place at that time. In addition, Civil War movie extras who worked on the 1993 film *Gettysburg*, a dramatization of the battle, claimed they had met and spoken to a man wearing a dirty Union Army uniform. This man left them with some musket rounds which they assumed were movie props but later turned out to be the real deal.

Other paranormal hotspots include Rose Farm, which served as a burial ground, and Pennsylvania Hall, which was a temporary hospital during the war. There has also been a sighting of a confederate soldier at the Cashtown Inn, which is about 8 miles away from the battlefield and was visited by the Confederates before they went into battle. Hummelbaugh House, located on the battleground, is said to be haunted by the disembodied screams of the ghost of Brigadier General William Barksdale of the Confederate Army, who died there from his battle wounds. The general's screams are sometimes accompanied by mysterious canine howling. This is believed to be the general's loyal hunting dog, who refused to budge from his grave or take any food and water and died there mournfully howling for his master.

Sach's Bridge, a covered bridge near Gettysburg battlefield where three Confederate soldiers were hanged as spies, has often been investigated by ghost hunters, some of whom have reported hearing gunfire and the sounds of horses' hooves. Others claim to have witnessed mysterious flickering lights or smelled cigar smoke, perhaps from defeated General Robert E. Lee of northern Virginia after the Union victory at Gettysburg.

There can be few places more violent and traumatic than a battlefield like Gettysburg, so it is perhaps unsurprising that there have been so many reports of unsettled spirits repeating their last steps on an eternal loop.

35. CRUMLIN ROAD GAOL

Crumlin Road Gaol, also known by its nickname, The Crum, was built in 1846, a short distance from Belfast city centre in Northern Ireland. As a Victorian-era prison, it is beautifully maintained for its historical and architectural significance. Despite its pleasant-looking exterior, it is believed to be one of the most haunted places in Ireland.

Crumlin served as a prison until 1996, and during that time there were seventeen executions and around 25,000 prisoners held there. It became a tourist attraction when it closed down and continues to attract thousands of visitors from all over the world.

Both staff and visitors at The Crum have reported mysterious encounters and experiences. These include doors opening and slamming shut by themselves, disembodied voices yelling for help and the apparition of a prisoner who walks down C wing and then vanishes. C wing is believed to be a paranormal hotspot, as it contains the famous condemned man's cell – a larger cell than others in the prison, it held a secret from its residents: an en suite hangman's noose, where the noose still hangs to this day.

In 2019, it was B wing that caught media attention in Belfast when a visitor took a photo of what appears to be a transparent man in uniform, with a chin strap to keep his hat in place, looking down a corridor. When the photo was taken, B wing was in total darkness and there was nobody there. B wing is also where the padded cell is located. Many visitors experience a sense of extreme dread when they enter the cell. The photo of one visitor who posed inside an empty coffin suggests they may not have been entirely alone, as there is supposedly a 'face in the coffin' lying beside him. D wing is not immune to reports of ghosts either, with some reports of objects moving inexplicably and the apparition of a man who stands in doorways and likes to observe the visitors.

The prison is connected by an underground tunnel to the Crumlin Road Courthouse, making transport of criminals from gaol to courthouse and back again safe and swift. The tunnel also has its fair share of reported hauntings. This includes the apparition of a grey man, and more recent ghost investigations have picked up on EVP recorders the muffled sounds of voices, moaning and crying when there is no explainable source.

Of the seventeen people executed in Crumlin, fifteen were buried within the gaol itself – and it seems their ghosts never left. Given the amount of trauma, death, suicide and intense emotions that happened within the walls, cells and tunnel of Crumlin, many believe some of the former prisoners simply can't move on. Not surprisingly, regular ghost tours and ghost investigations continue to take place. And for those brave enough to visit, be warned. The sight of the hangman's noose and a glimpse of the basement drop cell – the dreadful place where those who were hanged struggled frantically until they gasped their last breath – are known to routinely incite sudden feelings of panic.

36. WHALEY HOUSE

Any house built on the site of a former graveyard is likely to earn a reputation for being haunted, and this is most certainly the case for Whaley House in San Diego, which *Life* magazine once dubbed 'the most haunted house in America'.

Built in 1857 on the sombre site of not just a former burial ground but also a gallows, Whaley House is a two-storey Greek revival house that has had many reinventions over the past 150 years or so. It began as a family home but then transformed into a store house before becoming a county courthouse, then a theatre, then a ballroom, then a billiard hall and finally a school. In 1960, it opened as a museum.

The most well-known resident ghost at Whaley House is said to be Yankee Jim Robinson, who was hanged in 1852 from the gallows that once stood in the grounds. According to newspaper reports at the time, the execution was gruelling to watch. He was a heavyset man who fought for his life to the last, reportedly dragging his feet for as long as he could along the wagon as it moved away from the noose. When his feet finally lost contact, the momentum caused by his dragging action was so powerful that he swung backwards and forwards like an out-of-control swing, all the while gasping for breath as he slowly died.

Present at Yankee Jim's execution was a merchant and entrepreneur called Thomas Whaley, and, for some unfathomable reason, watching this gruesome spectacle did not put him off purchasing the site a few years later to build a family home. Construction began in May 1856, with Whaley stating, 'My new home, when completed, will be the handsomest, most comfortable and convenient place in town or within 150 miles of here.' The house was built from bricks created by Whaley's brickyard and furnished lavishly, costing more than $10,000. When it was completed, it was praised as the finest home in southern California.

However, Whaley's dream house turned into a nightmare, as within weeks of moving in, his family were petrified by the sounds of mysterious heavy footsteps, as if made by a large man wearing boots.

The family was also met with the tragic loss of their eighteen-month-old son Thomas, and the grief-stricken family moved out soon afterwards. But the heavy footsteps appear to have remained, and over the next century numerous residents and visitors continued to report hearing them. To this day, visitors to the museum still comment on ghostly footsteps from time to time. Perhaps Yankee Jim is still cursing the ground where he was executed. What's more, baby Thomas appears to have stayed nearby too, with visitors reporting the sounds of tiny footsteps, a baby's cries and even eerie giggles.

Some have claimed to see apparitions of the older members of the Whaley family too, as well as the ghost of an unknown woman wearing a long skirt in the area that used to be the courthouse. There has also been a report of a ghost dog, which is said to be the fox terrier owned by the Whaley family during their brief residence there.

One former employee at Whaley House reported seeing the apparition of a young girl in the dining area, which some suggest may be the ghost of a friend of the Whaley children called Anna Belle Washburn, although no records of her exist. The story goes that when playing outside, Anna ran into a clothes line and died of a broken neck. Thomas found her and placed her dead body in the dining room before it was taken away to be buried.

37. THE BRITISH MUSEUM

First established in 1753 and located in the Bloomsbury area of London, the British Museum is a public museum of human history and culture from ancient times to the present day. A permanent home for approximately 8 million relics and more than 6,000 human remains, it is one of the largest museums in the world.

Many of the relics, such as mummies, skulls, perfectly preserved bog bodies, battle weapons and statues of gods and goddesses, are potent symbols of death and the afterlife. Spending a night alone there would unnerve even the most sceptical among us. Not surprisingly, there have been reports from night guards of objects appearing and disappearing, unexplained strange sounds, and figures in the shadows when the doors are locked to the public and the lights go out. But it is not just during the night that these reports have occurred. During the day there have also been dozens of reports from both visitors and staff of eerie disembodied footsteps, locked doors opening by themselves, sudden temperature shifts and security alarms triggering for no logical reason.

On one quite literally striking occasion a guard was attempting to shut the heavy doors of the gallery that contains the Sutton Hoo helmet, which historians believe was worn by seventh-century King of East Anglia Raedwald. The guard was violently shoved to the ground by an invisible force he can't explain, and his strange fall was witnessed by his supervisor.

Shadowy figures and balls of light (orbs) have been glimpsed on security cameras and discovered on photographs taken by tourists. A group of Dutch tourists believed they could see the face of a little girl in a series of photos they took of the sixteenth-century German mechanical galleon. The girl appeared to be wearing sixteenth-century clothes.

The areas of the museum believed to be most awash with paranormal energy are the north and east stairwells at either end of the upper floor near the Egyptian gallery, which houses the famous mummies. One photograph taken by tourists of a young child reveals a looming dark shadow rising out of the floor as if to swallow the child. Security guards have also commented on temperature shifts in this gallery, with it being inexplicably cold even on hot summer nights.

The museum denies all possibility of paranormal presences. And many of the staff who have reported strange feelings of dread or being stared at, or who have encountered or experienced some of the spooky things mentioned above, do not believe in ghosts. What they and paranormal investigators do believe, however, is that it is possible some of the relics in the museum, particularly those associated with intense emotions and trauma, may somehow be imprinted with an energy that refuses to die.

38. SAVANNAH

There are many contenders for the most haunted city in the US, such as Salem, Massachusetts, due to its history of witchcraft. Then there are places such as Vicksburg in Mississippi (the scene of severe casualties during the Civil War), Alton in Illinois (a town that witnessed more than its fair share of natural disasters, murders, epidemics, civil war and tragedy), and Gettysburg in Pennsylvania (regarded as the scene of the bloodiest battle in the Civil War). These places seem permanently haunted by their brutal histories.

Every town, city and community in the US will have at least one ghost story or haunted home. But some have more than others, and a strong contender for the crown of America's most haunted is Savannah in Georgia due to the sheer number of ghost stories and reports of paranormal activity, not to mention the thriving industry of ghost and cemetery tours that take place all year round.

Paranormal hotspots include the Pirates' House, which is one of the most ancient buildings in the city, and Gribble House, where a series of axe murders occurred. However, it is Savannah's cemeteries that are perhaps most notorious. Bonaventure Cemetery, located beside the Wilmington River and famous for its photogenic magnolia, dogwood, live oaks and fascinating tombstones, is believed to be haunted by one of Savannah's most well-known resident ghosts – that of a six-year-old girl called Gracie Watson, who died of pneumonia in 1889. It is said that her crying ghost haunts the life-size statue that looms over her grave, with some saying they have seen her statue move or blink or even shed a solitary tear of blood.

Bonaventure has other eerie statues that are said to 'come alive' from time to time when visitors stand in front of them. There are also reports of disembodied babies, crying and giggling children, and phantom dogs barking.

Colonial Park Cemetery, located in the heart of Savannah's

historical district, was first used as a burial site in around 1750, and numerous apparitions and mysterious sounds have been reported there over the centuries. The ghost of a convicted murderer called Rene Rondolier, who was hanged from a tree inside the cemetery, is its most famous resident ghost and seriously scary at 7 feet tall, with some ghost hunters calling the cemetery 'Rene's playground'.

Laurel Grove Cemetery was established in 1853 and in the Civil War era was a segregated burial ground. There are two separate entrances, and the difference between the graves on each side is strikingly sad. But it is not just the unjust history of the place that stands out. There have been reports of a transparent woman floating aimlessly in her wedding gown, as well as a ghost train story that dates back to 1894. Whenever a railway car passed the cemetery on an old trolley line, the pitiful sound of a crying child was often heard coming from carriage 28, even though no crying child was in that carriage at the time.

Sorrel Weed House, which was built in the 1940s and appeared in the 1994 film *Forrest Gump*, is also thought to be home to at least two bitter ghosts whose shadowy silhouettes stalk the halls. These are believed to include the ghost of Matilda Sorrel, the wife of shipping merchant Francis Sorrel, who allegedly jumped to her death from the top floor of the house after discovering that her husband was having an affair. The word 'allegedly' is used for good reason, as documents show that by the time of her suicide, the Sorrel family were actually living in another property close by.

All this is just the tip of the ghostly iceberg when it comes to haunted Savannah, a city that, since it was first established in 1733, has endured harrowing disease outbreaks as well as fires and savage wars. It has had to rebuild itself time and time again. And whenever Savannah has successfully arisen from the ashes, it seems that ghosts have arisen and simply refused to leave too.

39. AKERSHUS FORTRESS

Situated beside the clear blue waters of the fjord in Oslo, Norway, is Akershus, a magnificent looming fortress which locals believe to be the most haunted place in Norway. Built in 1300, this medieval fortress has been the dwelling place of royalty and political leaders for centuries – and of the ghost stories that so often accompany them.

Although the castle has successfully guarded the capital city's inner harbour, it has seen its fair share of bloodshed. During the Second World War it was occupied by the Germans and savage executions took place there. It also served its time as a prison that was infamous for gruelling physical labour and the use of irons, chains and prisoner isolation as disciplinary techniques. Some believe that the trauma, injury and death this fortress has witnessed over the years may have imprinted itself energetically within the high walls. The prison closed in 1950, and Akershus Fortress is now a popular tourist attraction.

Over the decades there have been a number of reports from both guards and tourists of scratching sounds heard along the fortress walls and halls, as well as disembodied footsteps. Some have felt a force pushing their backs and heard invisible chains rattle along the hallways.

Perhaps the most terrifying ghost is Malcanisen (meaning 'vicious dog'), a cursed black dog with bloody jaws and flaming eyes believed to have been buried alive at the entrance of the fortress to bring the owners good luck. They miscalculated badly, as it is said the dog continues to haunt the castle gates today, howling at night and bringing bad luck to anyone who looks into its eyes.

Burning women, or nightpyres, are also believed to haunt the fortress. They are allegedly only seen when fires are lit in the castle and are described as small women with ugly grins and horrific laughter. There have been reports of screams, possibly from the people executed in the fortress, and the clicking hooves of a ghostly horse. A mysterious lady known as Mantelgeisten ('cloaked ghost') has also been encountered by many, suddenly appearing from the darkness. She wears a full-length robe and, chillingly, has no face.

40. PENNHURST STATE SCHOOL AND HOSPITAL

Opened in 1908 as the Eastern Pennsylvania Institution for the Feeble-Minded and the Epileptic, Pennhurst State School and Hospital in Spring City, Pennsylvania, was a place where the mentally ill were sent to be confined and treated in dubious, experimental and sometimes downright brutal ways.

Abuse was rife at Pennhurst. It was designed to be a small, self-sufficient community for around 500 patients, with its own shops, power plant, farm, hospital, school and morgue, but over time, serious overcrowding and a terrifying environment meant it came to resemble a concentration camp. Patients, many of whom were disabled children abandoned by their parents, or criminals or immigrants who could not speak English, were given labels such as 'imbecile' or 'insane' or 'epileptic' by the staff. They were subject to unimaginable neglect and cruelty, with staff restraining patients on beds for days without food and water or the opportunity to clean themselves. Drugging of patients was routine, and if any patient was troublesome, their teeth were removed – so much so that it was commonplace for visitors to find teeth in the corridors. It's no wonder the place later became known as 'the shame of Pennsylvania'. Pennhurst continued in its shame until 1968, when lawyers intervened to limit the possibility of abuse, but it didn't shut down for good until the late 1980s.

Given its dark and disturbing history, Pennhurst has become a magnet for reports of alleged paranormal activity and is rife with distressing ghost stories. Visitors report feelings of dread and being watched from behind, and some even hear disembodied cries of pain. There have also been reports of the sound of water rushing from taps, even though there are no bathroom fixtures in the building. Ghost hunts have been numerous at Pennhurst, and there is a collection of intriguing atmospheric photos, video footage and EVP recordings to consider. Shadowy figures have been seen, and some visitors have felt unseen hands pushing them from behind. Although most of the spirits at Pennhurst are believed to be friendly, if extremely distressed, that has not stopped reports of satanic worship at the property.

41. ST ANDREWS

St Andrew's in Fife, Scotland, is packed with ghosts. Famous for its golf, ancient university, cathedral and ruins, it also has a reputation among paranormal enthusiasts, which may have begun in earnest in 1911 with the publication of a book called *St Andrews Ghost Stories* by W. T. Linskill. The stories in the book entered local legend, and over the years other paranormal authors such as Richard Falconer have continued to revise and supplement the book, ensuring the spirit of Linskill's research never dies.

Arguably the most well-known and referenced St Andrew's ghost is the apparition of a white lady. She has been seen on several occasions over the past 200 years. She is always dressed entirely in white and is typically seen around the cathedral precinct or waving a handkerchief from a window at St Rule's Tower, known as the 'Chamber of Corpses'. Visitors should not confuse her handkerchief wave as a welcoming sign, as it is said she does not like guests coming near her 'lair', and many local residents avoid the area at night for fear of offending her. Unnervingly, in 1868 when stonemasons were refurbishing the tower, they discovered several coffins in a hidden sealed chamber. One of those coffins did not have a lid – and contained the skeleton of a woman wearing a white dress and white leather gloves.

St Andrews University may also have a resident ghost: a sixteenth-century student and teacher called Patrick Hamilton, who it seems has never left his residency. Hamilton was a Protestant reformer who was executed in February 1528 for heresy, burned at the stake on a bitterly cold day at the entrance of St Salvator's Chapel. However, because it was so cold, his execution took from midday until 6 p.m., as the executioners simply could not get the fires to the right heat and intensity. Even placing gunpowder under Hamilton's arms and on his face did not act as a catalyst for the flames to engulf him, though it did cause extreme injury. Eventually he died a martyr for the Reformation, and his last words were, 'Lord Jesus, receive my spirit.' The stone of the tower he was facing when he slowly burned is said to have the image of his face scorched into it.

Visitors to the execution site have reported the sound of disembodied screaming, as well as crackling sounds and the smell of burning flesh. St Andrews University students are warned not to step on the monogram which marks the spot of Hamilton's death, because if they do, they are said to be cursed and likely to fail their exams. The way to remove the curse is to run into the North Sea in the annual May dip at 5 a.m. For the other months of the year, stripping naked and running backwards three times around St Salvator's quad is believed to do the trick.

Another famous St Andrews ghost is the Veiled Nun of St Leonard's. She wears a black nun's habit and floats along Nun's Walk, which heads towards St Leonard's Kirk. The horrifying backstory is that a local girl was so devasted and heartbroken when her lover died that she mutilated herself so no man would ever fall in love with her again. She cut off her ears, eyelids and lips and branded her cheeks before joining a nunnery, where the injuries of her self-mutilation eventually grew septic and killed her. Still lurking today, for those unfortunate enough, she is said to slowly lift her veil to reveal her horrifically disfigured face to terrified passers-by.

Not all the ghosts of St Andrews are menacing, however. There have been reports of a kindly monk who appears on the ancient stairs of St Rule's Tower, and also of a ghost who is happy to retrieve lost balls on the Old Course. Some believe this may be the ghost of nineteenth-century golfer Tom Morris, who, from the young age of seventeen, won the Open Championship four times in a row. Tragically, on returning from a golfing event in 1875, he discovered that his young wife had died giving birth, and four months later he died of a broken heart.

There are hundreds of other reports of hauntings and ghosts to be found within the cobbled streets and medieval ruins of St Andrews, a most haunted location that quite rightly deserves a book of its own. St Andrews has a turbulent past well worth researching, and anyone who visits will sense that it is a place oozing mystery and haunted history from every pore.

42. OLD CHANGI HOSPITAL

Old Changi Hospital in Singapore was built as part of a military base in 1935. During the Japanese occupation, the hospital was used by the Japanese secret police – the Kempeitai – as a prison. The Kempeitai were notorious for their brutality and cruelty, including torture and executions. Rumours suggested that the hospital even had dedicated torture rooms, complete with chains and bloodstains on the wall.

When the Second World War ended, the building became a hospital again. By 1997, however, Old Changi was abandoned. It appears that the grisly spirit that was imprinted there during its time as a prison has remained. There have been many sightings by locals and visitors to the abandoned site of ghostly Japanese soldiers with bloody injuries. It is believed these are the ghosts of those who were executed there. There have also been reports of loud bangs, crashes and wild screams. The ghosts of those who died in the children's ward are believed to linger there too, as are the ghosts of former patients.

Only those with a brave heart should visit Old Changi. Visitors to the site have reported hearing mysterious footsteps and whispers, as well as feeling sudden changes in temperature and being touched or pushed by invisible hands. Feelings of dread are common, as are sightings of shadows moving independently. Several passers-by have also taken photographs and video footage (which can be viewed online) of what appear to be ghostly figures standing at the windows.

One of the most well-known Old Changi ghost stories is that of a nurse who was raped and murdered by Japanese soldiers in the hospital. She appears from time to time as a pale figure in a nurse's uniform, carrying towels and walking with purpose down the abandoned corridors. Another often reported ghost is that of a Japanese soldier who is believed to have committed hara-kiri (suicide) there.

43. THE JERSEY DEVIL

Once a thriving home to saw and paper mills and towns for those who worked in them during the Colonial period, the New Jersey Pine Barrens is a forest-heavy area in the US. Over time, the Pine Barren community relocated to nearby Pennsylvania with the discovery of coal there, leaving behind eerie ghost towns and the inevitable legends associated with them.

Although there are many fantastical stories associated with the Pine Barrens, the most famous is without doubt the so-called Jersey Devil. This entry could sit equally well in the Inhuman section of this book, given that the Jersey Devil resembles a mythical monster; however, I have chosen to include it as a residual haunting due to the fact that the story has a human origin, with the birth of a baby reportedly either so badly deformed that it repulsed its mother or so unwanted that it suffered intolerable neglect. Whatever the reason, the anguish and pain associated with the tragic birth created a lasting impression that has simply refused to die.

The story goes that a demonic-looking baby with hooves and wings was born in 1735 to Deborah 'Mother' Leeds, the wife of a rival to Benjamin Franklin – who may or may not have been responsible for the story gathering pace. It was her thirteenth child, and she was so tired of giving birth she cursed the child.

Some versions of the story say she was a witch, others that the child's father was the devil himself. Either way, the story refused to die, and by the late 1700s the baby was known as the Leeds Devil, either due to its connection with the Leeds family or to the South Jersey town where it all took place, Leeds Point.

Historians have suggested that the story may have originated from religious and political disputes that resulted in the influential Leeds family, whose crest had winged dragons on it, being described as 'monsters' rather than from any actual creature.

Real or not, over the centuries sightings of the monster have continued. The brother of Napoleon Bonaparte, Joseph Bonaparte, built a mansion in the Pine Barrens and allegedly saw the creature. In the 1840s, attacks on livestock were blamed on the beast and there were regular sightings of it in the area, often accompanied by mysterious howls and screams. The year 1909 was big for sightings, with newspapers publishing numerous eyewitness accounts of dramatic encounters in South Jersey and Philadelphia. The coverage was so extensive and impactful that several schools in the Delaware Valley closed and workers were encouraged to stay safe at home while courageous vigilantes searched in vain for the creature. There were further sightings in the 1950s, 1960s and beyond.

The Jersey Devil is sometimes said to sit beside a ghostly golden-haired girl who is dressed in white. The two apparitions together stare silently at the sea. The story goes that the Jersey Devil had a son who fell in love with a golden-haired rich girl. Her family would not allow the two to marry, so they sent her away. Heartbroken, she took her own life. This story again supports there being a very human origin to the haunting stories that have gathered around the so-called Jersey Devil.

To date there has been no hard evidence to support reports of the Jersey Devil or any other apparition haunting the Pine Barrens. But its fantastical legend stubbornly lives on in the frequent cameo appearances the creature makes to this day in fantasy books, movies and video games.

44. DALSTON HALL

Dalston Hall is a magnificent fifteenth-century mansion located in a picturesque village on the edge of the glorious Lake District in Cumbria, north-west England. Now a hotel rich in historical charm, although it serves as a tranquil retreat for some, the experience has also felt surreal for many due to the sheer number of ghostly sightings that have allegedly taken place there over the years.

Driving through the tree-lined entrance feels like crossing into a magical world, and at night the floodlit towers add to the sense of otherworldly enchantment. With over half a century of history behind it, not surprisingly this hotel has many a resident ghost. Some of the alleged apparitions reported there include 'Sad Emily', who has been spotted independently by several psychics looking downcast as she stands forlornly by the window in Room 4, her gaze always southward. She is said to wear a bonnet adorned with flowers and cotton frills, and her waist is tightly corseted. She also wears a ring which she plays with. All those who have seen her report experiencing feelings of deep sadness and longing, as if she is waiting endlessly for someone to return home.

Another apparition of a different young girl has also been reported at Dalston. This distressing figure is seen being dragged along the corridor by her hair, her pale, heavily powdered face suggesting she may have been born in the 1500s. It is possible she is the ghost of a courtesan who is thought to have been raped and thrown from the window to her death by a man wearing leather, whose ghost also seems to reside in the hall.

The apparitions of three women and a blonde girl have also been reported on the stairs at Dalston Hall. Creepily, they all stand still and simply watch people passing by. However, perhaps the most famous apparition reported at the hall is that of the doomed former English Queen, Lady Jane Grey, who visited Dalston Hall before her execution. Her ghost has been spotted walking solemnly in the gallery above the manor hall.

Strange sounds coming from the cellar when there is nobody there have also been reported, and psychics have sensed the presence of a looming, shadowy entity with long fingernails and the hint of a face, as well as that of a burly looking handyman who wears tweed trousers and an armband on his right arm. He appears to have loved his physical job of transporting barrels so much, he has never wanted to leave. A woman – possibly another former staff member – has also been said to haunt the grille at the bottom of the tower that leads into the hall.

Some ghost hunters believe that underneath the hall floor there is some kind of portal from this world to the next, a void that has now been bricked up but which still allows otherworldly beings through. The alleged hauntings that visitors have sensed, seen or heard at Dalston Hall, from reports of mysterious pipe music playing to sounds of a never-ending ghostly party, certainly show no signs of abating.

45. THE MYRTLES PLANTATION

The Myrtles Plantation, located around 70 miles north of New Orleans in Louisiana, attracts an endless stream of visitors every year, and many of them come in search of ghosts. According to the US tourist bureau, it is one of the most haunted places in America, and this description has further increased its reputation as a paranormal hotspot.

Ghost hunters are convinced that the key to discovering why this place is allegedly haunted must lie in its violent past imprinting its energy on the place. Since the plantation was built in 1794, no less than ten murders are said to have taken place there. This may, however, be an exaggeration. Research suggests it may only have been one murder – that of former owner William Winter – but records show that previous owners of the plantation had more than their fair share of violence, tragedy and trauma in their lives.

The most infamous ghost is Chloe, an enslaved governess who was hanged around the year 1820 for the murder of Sara Woodruff and her daughters, the wife and children of her master, who was also her lover. It is said that Chloe roams the manor at night and sometimes likes to unsettle guests by appearing or lifting the mosquito nets that surround their beds. Another ghost that is said to appear is that of William Winter, the owner of the plantation from 1860 to 1871, who was shot in the chest one night while relaxing on his porch. He managed to stagger into the house and climb seventeen of the twenty stairs before he died in his wife's arms. Allegedly, the sound of his dying body climbing to stair seventeen, where the noise stops, has been heard by staff and visitors alike.

Other notable sightings include the apparition of two little blonde girls who like to peer in through the windows of the house, startling unsuspecting guests; a confederate soldier who incessantly marches across the porch; and even a voodoo priestess who, according to lore, is eternally frustrated because her so-called powers could not save a young girl from a fatal disease. The ghost of a Native American woman has also been reported, perhaps because the manor may have been built over a Native burial ground.

The plantation also has a haunted mirror, which is believed to be cursed by the restless spirit of Sara Woodruff. To this day, visitors to the plantation feel unnerved in the mirror's presence. In addition, photographs taken at the plantation continue to surface that appear to show ghostly images trapped inside the mirror.

46. LA CASA MATUSITA

La Casa Matusita is an allegedly haunted house with a genuinely mind-blowing reputation for being a house of ultimate terror. It is situated in the middle of downtown Lima in Peru. Locals say that it is possible to lose your mind if you stay too long in the house. The apparent hauntings probably date back to its first resident and a belief that her vengeful ghostly presence simply refuses to leave the place, possessing those who dare to live there.

The house was built in the 1700s, and its first resident was a mystery to the locals. Dervaspa Parvaneh was of Persian ancestry and emigrated to Lima from Europe. As she had no connection to the area and practised as a healer, she soon became the subject of much local gossip. Eventually she was accused of witchcraft and of being in league with the devil and was executed. According to lore, as she was being burned alive at the stake, she loudly screamed and cursed the place of her death.

Several years later, her dreadful curse seems to have taken effect. A wealthy man who treated his servants with cruel disdain met his just deserts, quite literally. One day when he was hosting a dinner party, the servants put hallucinogens in the food and drink as an act of revenge for their mistreatment. They then hid, waiting in the kitchen to see what would happen. They had no idea what horror awaited them.

On hearing screams, when the servants re-entered the dining room, they saw that the hallucinogens had had an unexpectedly violent effect. They found a total bloodbath, with bodies lying everywhere, many of which were decapitated and mutilated. The walls were painted in blood. The scene was so grotesque, it sent the servants mad, and they were admitted to the city's asylum.

About a century later, La Casa Matusita witnessed another gruesome tragedy. The Matusita family – a Japanese family from which the house takes its current name – were initially content living in the house. However, this was the calm before the storm, as the dark energy lurking in the house seems to have taken hold. Mr Matusita, a fiercely jealous man, lost the plot one day when he returned home and found his wife in bed with another man. Seeing red, he grabbed a knife from the kitchen and killed his wife and her lover. He then killed his children and himself.

The house's reputation for driving its residents mad gathered further steam in the 1970s, courtesy of an Argentine TV presenter called Humberto Vilchez Vera, who declared he would spend an entire week living, working and sleeping in the house to prove it was not haunted. The house appears to have got the better of him. After just four hours, he emerged wildly disorientated and babbling nonsense. In the years following, he was in and out of psychiatric facilities, and for the rest of his life he would never speak of what he had experienced in those few hours he spent at the dreaded La Casa Matusita.

Ghost hunters have investigated the house and more often than not linked its dark energy to the first owner. Priests have also unsuccessfully attempted exorcisms there. One theory has suggested that because the old US Embassy in Peru was close by, the legend of La Casa Matusita was fabricated to keep anyone from entering and spying on the embassy from there. Whether or not this was the case, the legend has persisted long after the embassy moved away.

47. FAIRFIELD HILLS HOSPITAL

Fairfield State Hospital, known as Fairfield Hills Hospital after 1963, was once a psychiatric hospital in Newtown, Connecticut, which admitted and treated patients from 1933 through to 1995. It was owned and operated by the State of Connecticut Department of Mental Health, and although originally intended for around 500 patients, at one point it was treating around 4,000. Many of the patients sent to Fairfield were criminals deemed to be insane.

Treatments at Fairfield Hills, now considered inhumane and deadly, included insulin shock therapy, electroconvulsive therapy, psychosurgery, hydrotherapy and frontal lobotomy. A series of concrete tunnels connected different buildings, and these tunnels were in constant use for conveying food, medicine and corpses from one area of the overcrowded and understaffed hospital to another. Mysterious deaths, suicides and stories of abuse were rife when the hospital was in operation. For example, in 1941, an autopsy of a patient who suddenly died revealed that the man had been beaten to death. There were also numerous complaints about medical staff being drunk while on duty.

Over the years, due to its ugly past and unauthorized and cruel treatments, Fairfield has understandably gained a reputation for being seriously haunted and has attracted the interest of paranormal enthusiasts and TV shows. Disembodied voices of wailing and anguish have been heard time and time again, and it is thought they may be the ghosts of former patients who died in agony due to the ghastly experimental nature of the treatments there. There have also been reports of apparitions of people dressed in white, presumably former employees of the hospital.

Before they were closed to the public for health and safety reasons, the tunnels that connected the sixteen buildings that comprised the hospital were allegedly a magnet for paranormal activity, with visitors reporting hearing the sound of scratching on the walls and the clinking of medical instruments, as well as moaning and crying. Access to Fairfield is virtually non-existent today, with large warning and keep-out signs everywhere. Those who do visit report feeling inexplicably cold and nauseous, with those unpleasant feelings only passing when they leave the building.

48. ALLERTON TOWER

Allerton Tower is an abandoned and rather creepy-looking manor house situated in Allerton Towers public park in Liverpool, England. Dating back to the eleventh century, it has understandably had numerous owners. In the eighteenth and nineteenth centuries, it was owned by a family of railway magnates, but when they left the manor, there was nobody wealthy enough to be able to manage the upkeep. Over the years it has been slowly left to deteriorate and gather dust and, of course, to become overrun with ghosts , according to Tom Sleman, author of the *Haunted Liverpool* book series. One of the most well-known is the so called 'grey lady' of Allerton Tower.

In the 1850s, Allerton Tower was owned by railway director Sir Hardman Earle. Earle had a large family which included three sons. There were persistent rumours about Sir Hardman being corrupt and ruthless. According to local lore, one compelling backstory involves Earle's youngest son, William, who visited a local tavern with his brothers and, as the night progressed, fell in love at first sight with a local Irish girl called Mary. As she was not of the same social standing as William, his brothers pulled him away from her and told him never to see her again. William ignored his brothers and continued to meet Mary in secret. The loved-up couple made secret plans to elope.

It was only a matter of time before Sir Hardman found out about William's secret. He exploded with rage and beat his son black and blue before locking him in a room. William's brothers visited Mary and told her she had to stay away from William for good. Mary burst into tears and told them she was pregnant with William's child and she had already told her uncle about the baby. She begged them for help.

William's brothers decided they could not risk Mary's pregnancy humiliating their family, and they also feared Mary's uncle would try to blackmail them. So they hatched a plot to kill both Mary and her uncle. A few days later, they lured Mary to a secluded spot under the pretence of wanting to help her. Instead, they savagely beat her and her unborn child to death. The brothers carried Mary's mangled body across a field and dropped it into an old well. The following night, Mary's uncle was killed by a horse ridden by a man wearing a black coat and a hat that covered his face.

Mary's body was discovered a day or so later, and given that her uncle had also died suddenly, the locals had their suspicions that this was a double murder. A local fortune teller led them to Allerton Tower, where they were met by Hardman Earle, who was wielding a loaded shotgun. With no proof, the villagers dissipated. It seemed that the family had got away with murder, but a few weeks later an apparition of Mary covered in blood and wounds, soaking wet and pointing her finger accusingly at them, allegedly appeared simultaneously in the two brothers' bedrooms. After seeing this apparition, neither brother had a good night's sleep again and they slowly lost their minds. Mary's ghost was also said to appear to Sir Hardman Earle on his deathbed, no doubt hastening his demise. She also allegedly appeared – this time in a loving and calming way – to her lover William the evening before his death in 1885. From then onwards, the apparition of a pale and beautiful pregnant lady has been reported many times haunting the ruins of Allerton Tower.

49. POVEGLIA ISLAND

A small island situated between Venice and Lido in the Venetian Lagoon of northern Italy, Poveglia is divided into two distinct parts by a small canal. Records show the island was first inhabited in AD 421 and remained so until 1379, when residents were forced to leave due to war. Poveglia is believed by some paranormal experts to be the most haunted island in the world – if not the most haunted location in the world.

For around a century after 1776, the building in the main part of the island was transformed into a quarantine for the plague- and disease-ridden. Many who were sent there died, and their bodies were burned on huge pyres. In the 1800s, the building was used as an asylum rife with experimental treatments for mental patients, such as lobotomies. One doctor working in the hospital in the 1930s is said to have jumped off the bell tower in a fit of despair, claiming he had been driven mad by the island's ghosts. The asylum was closed in 1968 and remained vacant despite plans to reinvent it. Visits to the island are limited and locals avoid it quite literally like the plague it was once used for, with those who fish in nearby waters often refusing to go near it for fear of being cursed.

Remaining buildings on the eerie island consist of a derelict church, a hospital, an asylum, a bell tower, housing and administrative buildings – and remains of plague pits where it is estimated around 150,000 bodies may have been buried.

Given its history and isolated location, it's not surprising that the island is a favourite place for ghost hunters and paranormal

TV shows to investigate and discuss. Those who do manage to visit it have reported seeing shadowy people lingering in the corners of their eyes and faces on the walls of the former asylum, as well as blood-curdling disembodied screams. Perhaps the most compelling evidence is that those who are courageous enough to set foot on the island are always eager to leave. Typically, they report feeling an inexplicable sense of anger and of being watched by a menacing presence.

50. HAM HOUSE

Ham House and gardens, situated on the banks of Richmond-upon-Thames in Surrey, England, is a red-brick mansion and one of Europe's best-preserved examples of seventeenth-century architectural grandeur. However, the mansion's opulent exterior conceals many ghostly secrets.

The Duchess of Lauderdale, Elizabeth Murray, who inherited the house from her father in 1655, often based herself at Ham House. It is believed to be the permanent residence of at least fifteen ghosts, including the duchess herself and her dog. Towards the end of her life, Elizabeth, an ambitious and ruthless soul, was confined to her bedroom due to her failing health, and this room in particular is said to be deeply haunted.

Many visitors have reported feeling a chilling presence there, with some even claiming to see a lady in black, presumably Elizabeth, quietly watching them as she stands on the nearby stairs. Staff working at Ham House also report an oppressive, strange atmosphere in Elizabeth's room, with some saying, 'Good afternoon, your ladyship,' when they enter it for fear of offending her with their uninvited presence. Others have detected the mysterious scent of roses – a scent associated with the duchess in her lifetime – but it is the mirror in this allegedly haunted room that is most feared. Some people say they feel they are being watched when they look into it, and staff members avoid looking into it at all. It's not just the mirror that is believed to be watching: there is a painting on the wall of the duchess when she was a young woman that seems to follow people with forever-watchful eyes.

The ghost of the duchess's dog – a King Charles spaniel – also appears never to have left Ham House. There have been sightings of the dog's apparition running along the galleries of the house. In addition, some visitors detect the smell of cigars even though smoking is not allowed in the house – the duchess's second husband was partial to a cigar or two after dinner.

Another ghostly presence that has been seen and sensed by visitors, staff and ghost hunters is that of a tragic servant called John McFarlane. He fell in love with a maidservant who jilted him.

Heartbroken, he jumped to his death from a top-floor window. The story goes that before he took his life, McFarlane scratched the date 1780 and his name on a pane of glass which can still be viewed today. His undead spirit has been seen trudging up and down the terrace.

The ghosts of Ham House have now very much become part and parcel of its rich history. Although these ghostly experiences can feel unsettling at times, they are never frightening, and for the most part the ghosts seem to be very much trapped in their own time, re-enacting the routines or traumas of their past. Or, in the case of the ever-watchful eyes of the duchess in black, calmly observing the intrusion of the present.

51. LIZZIE BORDEN HOUSE

Located at 92 Second Street, Fall River, Massachusetts, and now operating as a bed and breakfast, Lizzie Borden House is believed to be haunted by former resident Lizzie Borden herself.

The backstory is deeply troublesome but endlessly fascinating for paranormal experts and curious visitors who continue to flock to the house hoping to find answers. Before the clock struck noon on 4 August 1892, Lizzie is said to have brutally murdered her stepmother, Abby Durfee Gray, with an axe, and about an hour later she also allegedly killed her father, Andrew Borden, with the same weapon. Abby's battered body was found between the bed and the bureau in the guest room and Andrew's body was found with his head resting on the sofa arm next to the door in the downstairs sitting room.

It's an understatement to say that the Borden family was not a happy one, and although Lizzie was never convicted for the double murder due to lack of evidence at her trial and her claim that an intruder was responsible, there is every reason to believe she was guilty. Afterwards she remained in the Fall River area and started a new life under the name of Lizbeth until her death in 1927.

After Lizzie's death, the Second Street house remained private property for several decades until it was converted into a bed and breakfast. Guests who stay there can request to sleep in Lizzie's former bedroom and experience guided tours of the murder scenes in the downstairs sitting room where Andrew's bloody body was found and the bedroom where Abby was discovered.

With the house a permanent witness to an unsolved and unavenged double murder, it is small wonder that over the years it has reportedly been haunted by the ghosts of the Bordens. Guests, staff and paranormal investigators have experienced feelings of inexplicable, intense fear and dread, as well as sudden cold draughts and chills, always a sign that a ghostly presence may be nearby. There have also been accounts of doors opening and closing by themselves, unexplained footsteps and whispers, sightings of the full-blown apparition of Abby making beds in the guest rooms, and of the bloodied bodies of Abby and Andrew, apparently still lying undisturbed in the places they were found on that fatal day in 1892.

52. BALLYGALLY CASTLE

Northern Ireland's Ballygally Castle in County Antrim is believed to be haunted by the ghost of another doomed woman, formerly known as Lady Isabella Shaw.

The castle is now a thriving hotel, and guests who stay there tend to remark on its 'spooky' atmosphere more than any other allegedly haunted hotel. It was built by James Shaw, a Scottish immigrant, in 1635 in the style of a French château and has walls several feet thick. During the 1641 rebellion, the castle was attacked numerous times.

James Shaw's wife, Lady Isabella, came to live in the castle following their marriage. She was only sixteen when she first arrived at the castle, and the fate that awaited her there was a distressing one. Her husband was possessive and cruel, an alcoholic prone to fits of rage – so she often sought refuge from him on the battlements of the castle, hoping to catch a glimpse of her beloved Scottish homeland.

James was keen for Isabella to bear him a son, and it appears that this was the purpose of their marriage. It certainly wasn't for love, as he treated her worse than a servant. When Isabella fell pregnant and delivered a healthy baby girl, his disappointment and fury knew no bounds. He ordered his guards to drag his wife and newborn daughter to the turret room of the castle, where they were locked up and barely given enough food and drink to survive.

One cold night, Isabella could bear her punishment no longer and jumped to her death out of the window of the turret with her daughter in her arms. Another version of the Lady Isabella story is that she was having an affair and the daughter she bore was clearly not her husband's. This caused him to murder them both by pushing them from the castle turrets. Either way, Lady Isabella's room (otherwise known as the 'Ghost Room') has been well preserved for visitors who want to walk up the spiral staircase and see the view she might have seen just before her death. It is said that the cries of the baby can be heard to this day, and guests have reported knocks on their doors, believed to be Lady Isabella; when they answer, there is nobody there. There have also been sightings of her in a long, flowing, ivory-coloured silk dress which resembles a wedding dress, as that may have been the last day Isabella felt any true happiness. However, those who look carefully have noticed that they can see spots of blood staining the silk.

There appears to be another silk-dress-wearing apparition at Ballygally Castle, known as Madam Nixon and believed to be a woman who lived in the castle during the nineteenth century. The sound of her dress rustling has been heard in the corridors at night, and she has been seen in the castle turrets. Several guests staying at the Ballygally Castle Hotel have experienced other mysterious things over the years, including an inexplicable creeping green mist and the feeling of a presence standing in their room or watching them as they try to go to sleep.

53. DALHOUSIE CASTLE

Dalhousie Castle, once seat of the Ramsay clan, is one of Scotland's most ancient castles, dating back to the thirteenth century. It is still inhabited by the living, and apparently by the dead too.

Only the vaults and heavyset walls at the foundation level remain of the original castle. Although there is a spiral staircase leading down to the dungeon keep, it is said that prisoners were once lowered into the castle dungeon by a rope, making it impossible for them to escape or see the light of day again. Entry to the castle itself used to be via a drawbridge over a moat, but that was removed when the castle was transformed into a hotel.

A 'grey lady', believed to be lovelorn Lady Catherine, allegedly haunts the castle. According to reports, she died of a broken heart when she was just sixteen after being banished to the castle in 1695 when she was caught making love to a stablehand. Images of the teenager have allegedly been caught on camera and can be viewed online. Other versions of the story suggest that Lady Catherine was in fact the mistress of one of the Ramsay lairds, and when his wife discovered the affair, she imprisoned Catherine in one of the towers and left her to starve to death. Either way, she now haunts the towers, stairs, main corridor and dungeons. Said to be a very active ghost, she has been known to tap on the shoulders of guests, and some have woken to find her sitting at the end of their bed.

It's not just jilted women who are said to haunt the castle. The ghost of Sir Alexander Ramsay is also believed to linger forever in the castle halls and grounds. He was abducted and starved to death in 1400 when attempting to defend the castle from the King. Today, his harmless spirit makes itself known by creeping up on guests unseen and pulling their hair.

Because the ghostly activity is so rife at the hotel, ghost tours now happen at Dalhousie Castle on a regular basis, allowing individuals to see some of the spooky sights for themselves – but guests who have no part in the ghost tours have also experienced spooky happenings, including unexplained noises, moving objects and footsteps in the night.

Some surveys have suggested that Dalhousie is perhaps the number-one otherworldly stay in Britain.

54. THE HAY-ADAMS HOTEL

The Hay-Adams Hotel in Washington DC in America allegedly has a resident ghost whose past has decisively imprinted itself on the place.

Opened in 1929, it is a luxurious hotel and a favourite place for celebrities to stay. The ghost of Clover Adams – the sociable wife of writer Henry Adams who some believe was the inspiration for Henry James's famous novel *The Portrait of a Lady* – is said to haunt the hotel. During the 1870s, Clover, Henry Adams and their neighbours John Hay and his wife Clara were celebrated couples of their day. Hay was private secretary to Abraham Lincoln and both couples enjoyed a very active and elite social life, holding parties to which the likes of celebrated author Mark Twain were invited.

Clover loved to take photographs when she was alive – photography was her passion. However, when her beloved father died, she lost the will to live and took her own life by swallowing the potassium cyanide she used in her photographic work. The house Clover lived in was eventually demolished along with the neighbouring house inhabited by the Hays, and the Hay-Adams Hotel was built and opened.

Over the years several guests to the hotel have reported uncanny things happening during their stay, such as lights switching on and off for no reason and doors opening and closing by themselves. A peculiar smell lingers with her spirit too, faintly smelling of almonds, and the hotel's chandeliers are said to sway of their own accord. Some have glimpsed the fully realized ghostly figure of a woman, and staff have felt her friendly presence as they go about their work.

POLTERGEIST

'Mary stood near the door with her candle
in her hand, holding her breath.
Then she crept across the room, and, as
she drew nearer, the light attracted
the boy's attention and he turned his
head on his pillow and stared at her,
his gray eyes opening so wide
that they seemed immense.
"Who are you?" he said at last in a half-
frightened whisper. "Are you a ghost?"
"No, I am not," Mary answered, her own whisper
sounding half frightened. "Are you one?"'

The Secret Garden,
Frances Hodgson Burnett

Steven Spielberg's 1982 *Poltergeist* movie brought the term a lot
of recognition, but of course they have been around far longer
than that.

Rightly or wrongly, for many people the word 'poltergeist' is
synonymous with the words 'ghost' and 'haunting'. However, in
contrast to ghosts and hauntings, which have been mainstream
terms since ancient times, the word poltergeist didn't enter the

conversation about paranormal phenomena until it was introduced by paranormal scholar Catherine Crowe. In 1848, Crowe published *The Night Side of Nature: or Ghosts and Ghost Seers*, which was one of the first documented chronicles of mysterious experiences science struggled to explain and included stories about deathbed visions, apparitions and ghosts.

Dickens described *The Night Side* as 'one of the most extraordinary collections' of documented supernatural experiences ever written. Of Mrs Crowe, he wrote, 'She can never be read without pleasure and profit, and can never write otherwise than sensibly and well.' The book was a publishing sensation, but sadly Crowe seems to have suffered from mental health problems and disappeared from public view before her death in 1872 at the age of eighty-two. She left behind her a lingering and influential legacy for the future of paranormal research, most especially through her assured use of two German words, doppelgänger and poltergeist, which from then onwards entered popular paranormal vernacular.

A very noisy ghost

Doppelgänger is a combination of the words *doppel*, meaning 'double', and *gänger*, meaning 'goer': a living person's double. Meanwhile, poltergeist is made from *poltern*, 'to knock', and *geist*, 'spirit'. This equates to a poltergeist being an invisible noisy or troublemaking ghost capable of making loud sounds, such as knocking on windows and doors, and moving physical objects from one place to another. They can also create unpleasant smells, interfere with electricity and trip people up or even hit them. In most cases it is not a location, building or place that they haunt or attack but one specific person. There are records of ghosts tormenting their victims that date back to ancient Rome.

Poltergeist activity has been put forward as a possible explanation for alleged hauntings. Until the nineteenth century, such experiences were blamed on vengeful ghosts, spirits, demons, witches and the devil himself, and the clergy were called in for exorcisms. But more often than not, modern researchers believe that ghosts or spirits are not causing the activity. Psychological factors, such as delusions or hallucination, or environmental factors, such as air currents or underwater systems, or straightforward fraud are believed to be more convincing explanations. Another theory is that poltergeist activity has nothing to do with the dead and everything to do with the living, perhaps caused by unconscious psychokinesis on the part of the living, called the agent. This theory was originally put forward in the 1930s by psychical researcher and parapsychologist Nandor Fodor.

Psychokinesis

Psychokinesis (PK) is the alleged ability to influence physical objects using the power of thought. It is mind over matter. It sounds like the stuff of science fiction, but there is emerging credible research to suggest that this type of kinetic energy may exist. Studies on energy healing or reiki and the power of prayer, for example, are yielding thought-provoking results.

If you are a fan of the hit series *Stranger Things*, the lead character Eleven has PK ability. She can move objects and people by focusing her thoughts on them, and the more intense the emotions are when she has these thoughts, the more powerful her ability. Indeed, the most common human agent for a poltergeist is often a teenage girl similar to the character Eleven in age and in her experience of emotional turmoil. There will be some kind of internal anger related to stress within the family. However, unlike Eleven, who is aware of her abilities, the human agent in a poltergeist attack is often unconscious of her ability to move things by kinetic energy and has no idea she is the source of the disturbance.

In a typical poltergeist attack, many of the disturbances closely resemble a typical haunting. Mysterious things happen with no explainable cause, such as knocking, objects moving or flying by themselves, doors slamming, or lights switching on and off, prompting those involved to feel scared and confused and to suspect a haunting. In rare cases, physical assaults such as scratching and biting are reported, but studies show that most poltergeist activity involves the movement of small and large objects and rapping sounds. Although the most common cases involve young women going through the physical and emotional changes that accompany puberty, there have also been documented cases of it happening to adults and to both boys and men.

Whenever there are strong currents of emotional energy imprinting themselves on an atmosphere, as we discovered in the previous section on residual hauntings, this can allegedly act as a magnet for ghostly phenomena. And in almost all poltergeist cases, uncanny things that can't easily be explained away by the living can also occur. In short, PK can't explain away everything. And there are also those who believe that the theory of spirits of the dead causing poltergeist activity has been seriously overlooked.

Mind over matter

The notion that ghosts and poltergeists are one and the same persists. Popular books, TV shows and blockbuster horror movies have strengthened the connection. But as you read this next section, as enticingly supernatural as it all appears, please be aware that poltergeist activity, perhaps more than the other three categories, may not be about the potential of ghosts existing. Some parapsychologists believe they have absolutely no connection to ghosts or spirits at all. Instead, they have every connection to the person or people involved, and these individuals might perhaps benefit more from therapy or counselling than from any ghost investigation. It is also worth pointing out that many of the world's most famous and revisited poltergeist cases happened in the 1950s and 1960s, a time of radical reinvention and a trend towards mainstreaming what had previously appeared out of this world, perhaps due to the unprecedented horrors of the two world wars.

Despite all this, in every single one of the cases that follow, even those where rational explanations seem likely, some aspect of the story always remains entirely unexplained and continues to defy rational explanation.

What follows is a collection of some of the most well-reported poltergeist cases to date.

Read on with caution. Your thoughts are powerful. Make your own mind up. What do you sense is really going on here?

55. THE ENFIELD POLTERGEIST

It all began on the night of 30 August 1977, when Janet, aged eleven, and her younger sibling went to sleep in their bedroom in 284 Green Street, Enfield, North London. Their beds started to jolt up and down, but when the children ran screaming to their mother, Peggy, the bed-rocking stopped. The following night the children were awoken again from their sleep, but this time by a moving chair. Peggy took the chair downstairs. She returned to the children in their bedroom and all heard loud bangs coming from the walls and witnessed a chest of drawers shuffling by itself into the centre of the room. The frightened family fled to their next-door neighbour's house.

The neighbours initially didn't believe them and went into the house to investigate for themselves. They heard loud banging too and called the police, who on arrival also witnessed the moving chair. The following day Lego pieces and marbles started to fly across the room, so the family decided to contact the press.

A reporter from the *Daily Mirror* arrived and took photographs of the alleged paranormal activity. The newspaper called the Society for Psychical Research to investigate, and they sent North London resident and respected psychical researcher and inventor Maurice Grosse to investigate. Grosse began his investigation of the home on 5 September, a week after the disturbances had first begun.

In the first few days of his investigation he witnessed the moving chair in Janet's bedroom while she was sleeping. Other strange things happened one after another, and for the next two years Grosse extensively investigated the home, documenting in detail moving objects, flying toys, unexplained noises and even the children levitating. There is a famous image online of Janet's alleged levitation. Over thirty eyewitnesses (including neighbours, psychic researchers, journalists and even the local lollipop lady) saw and heard paranormal activity, with Janet often acting as the conduit for a mysterious gruff voice known as 'Bill'. In the end, Grosse had seen enough and was convinced the case was largely genuine. His colleague, the writer Guy Lyon Playfair, came to the same conclusion.

It is significant that this case involved young and adolescent children. It is also significant that there was internal family tension. Peggy was having problems getting over her divorce from the children's father. The children were struggling to process their new situation too, and according to the PK explanation for poltergeist activity, this made them prime candidates for being human agents.

Publicity-seeking trickery is a possible explanation, and this was the conclusion two other investigators sent by the Society of Psychical Research came to – Anita Gregory and John Beldoff. They were entirely unconvinced by the family. Indeed, hidden video cameras in the house did show Janet and her siblings jumping up and down on the bed and talking in a muffled voice like a ventriloquist.

The 2016 movie *The Conjuring 2* is based on the investigation into the Enfield case in 1978 by famous American paranormal investigators Ed and Lorraine Warren, who were both convinced there was a demonic explanation. A few years before, in January 1971, the Warrens had come to the same diabolic conclusion after investigating a series of unfortunate events endured by the Perron family in the States when they moved into a roomy farmhouse in Harrisville, Rhode Island. The experiences of the Perron family echoed those experienced here and inspired the first *Conjuring* movie.

Playfair and Grosse agreed with the Warrens' assessment and

maintained their conviction that an 'entity' was to blame, but both did question at some point whether there might also have been some trickery and exaggeration involved. In September 1978, the peculiar happenings stopped just as suddenly as they had started. Peggy continued to live in the house until her death.

The Enfield poltergeist was one of the first paranormal cases to truly capture the world's attention and show that hauntings don't just happen in stately homes and castles; they can happen in an ordinary council home too. As a result of being in the spotlight for a year, there was ample time for investigation, making it an incredibly well-documented case. A variety of explanations have been put forward, from those who believe it was a genuine poltergeist attack to those who suggest environmental factors, such as electromagnetic fields and gas pollution. But the general consensus today is perhaps best summed up by British psychology professor Chris French. In a 2016 feature for *Time Out* magazine, French argued that the case was most likely a hoax, given the fact that eyewitnesses can be impressionable and unreliable and exhibit confirmation bias – seeing what they are expected to see – and the children were probably involved in a school prank that just got way out of hand.

It is possible this famous poltergeist case did perhaps begin with and involve some unexplained phenomena. But whether it did or not has been obscured by the likelihood of it developing into fraud over time, perhaps when the children and their mother Peggy began to enjoy the attention they got from the investigation and the media.

56. THE INDIANAPOLIS POLTERGEIST

The Indianapolis poltergeist is another case that received a great deal of media interest and even saw the intervention of the local police department.

On 11 March 1962, a few minutes after 10 p.m. at 2910 North Delaware Street in Indianapolis, a series of unusual and unwanted events began that made both local and then national news. These included objects moving of their own accord, terrifying loud bangs, and smashing glasses and coffee cups. The events were so alarming that the three female residents of the house fled to stay overnight in a nearby hotel.

Renate Beck was a local restaurant operator who had moved into what was then a four- bedroom, two-bathroom home. She was Vienna-born and brought her thirteen-year-old daughter Linda and her argumentative and diabetic German mother Lina Gemmecke to live with her. It appears that the three ladies did not get on very well, with neighbours reporting hearing raised and often angry voices coming from their home.

Renate had just divorced and was hoping to begin afresh in a quiet area that would be a secure place to raise her daughter and care for her mother's failing health. However, when the family returned to the house from the hotel the next day, hoping the bizarre happenings that drove them away would not be repeated, they were disappointed. Glasses continued to smash by themselves, objects continued to move, and the disturbances escalated to the point Renate called the Indianapolis police to ask for their help.

In the coming days, interest in the paranormal disturbances grew. Some speculated that the smashing glasses was due to pranks – a pellet gun – or soundwaves in the area. Police officers were mystified when they too heard crashing coming from the empty upstairs of the house and alarming bruising and bite marks appeared on the three women. Private investigations chronicled a host of poltergeist activity, including feathers ripped from pillows and cutlery with a life of its own. On one occasion, a police officer walking out of an empty room was badly bruised by a flying glass.

These wild things continued for a few days until Lina was discovered throwing objects when she thought no one was looking. By then the house was in total chaos. Lina was arrested for causing a disturbance, but Renate fiercely defended her mother, saying she was having a diabetic attack triggered by the anxiety caused by the poltergeist activity. Unsure what to do in this unprecedented case, the police offered Lina a deal. If she returned immediately to her homeland in Germany, all charges would be dropped. She accepted.

Both the police and the media were satisfied that the incidents had been caused by the women themselves, but a family friend stated that he and his wife had witnessed crazy things happening that the women could not have possibly caused. Although questions remain about the accuracy of the story and the exact nature and cause of the unusual events that took place, it does appear at first glance that the Indianapolis poltergeist is an open and shut case of fraud probably perpetuated by Renate's mother, Lina.

Or was it an example of unconscious psychokinetic energy? Perhaps young Linda was the human agent. Or was it the work of Renate herself? She was suffering from the combined stress of both her recent divorce and the move to a new house in a new area, as well as caring for the needs of her demanding mother and adolescent daughter.

Whatever really happened, all three women were emotionally conflicted. They were not getting along well with each other either, making the three of them a magnet for stress and unhappiness and a recipe for potential poltergeist activity.

57. THE THORNTON HEATH/ CROYDON POLTERGEIST

The Thornton Health poltergeist case happened in a normal terraced home in Thornton Heath in Croydon, London, in 1938. The alleged poltergeist activity clustered around a woman called Alma Fielding, who owned the house at the time. The exact location of the house, however, remains unknown.

Hungarian-born British–American parapsychologist Nandor Fodor investigated the case. Fodor proposed the theory that poltergeists are external manifestations of inner tension and emotional conflicts, rather than independent supernatural entities possessing the victim. He believed that the mysterious disturbances were unconsciously being caused by the human agent's mind. In the case of the Thornton Health poltergeist, he believed it was caused by repressed trauma that Fielding had endured as a child.

From the first few days of investigating the case, Fodor suspected that Alma was behind the poltergeist activities, which included flying objects, items appearing and disappearing, glasses smashing, and choking marks mysteriously appearing around her neck. At one point, after hearing creaking footsteps throughout the house, Alma's son woke in the middle of the night to find an old man in his room, apparently angry that the family was trespassing in his property. Fodor examined Alma's psychological background and discovered that she had a history of hysteria and dissociated personality disorder, which included hearing voices. He was convinced she was neurotic with a disordered personality and that she was hiding the objects in her clothing and self-harming.

In a moment that would be judged harshly in terms of ethical practices today, his suspicions were proved correct when one day after she fainted, an intimate search of her clothing revealed small household objects hidden in her bra. It seems that Alma was indeed fabricating at least some of the paranormal activity surrounding her.

This event was enough to convince Fodor that Alma was fabricating the hauntings and enjoying deceiving others and the attention it brought her. He did, however, state how important he felt her case was because it offered a new direction for psychical research – one that hoped to better understand the mental and emotional patterns that may accompany such cases, even if the cases were eventually proved to be fraudulent. He did not believe Alma was mad or consciously aware of what she was doing.

The Thornton Health poltergeist case did not reach public consumption until 1958, when Fodor finally published his findings in the *Journal of Clinical Psychopathology* and a book. The reason it took so long after the event was the fierce criticism he received from his peers – most notably his fellow psychical researchers, who could not agree entirely with his focus on the psychological explanation for all alleged poltergeist cases. Indeed, he was dismissed from his research post at the International Institute for Psychical Research because of it. He was also attacked in the spiritualist newspaper *Psychic News*, which he sued for libel.

Detractors argued that Fodor did not have enough proof and jumped far too quickly to his psychological conclusion. For example, he did not take into account inconsistencies such as when Alma was studied at a college by Fodor and strange things continued to happen in her absence at home, suggesting the haunting was associated with the location rather than Alma. Despite this, Fodor's theory for poltergeist activity – and the importance of greater empathy and understanding of the inner conflict the human agent may be experiencing – eventually won the recognition it deserved. For Alma and her family, however, the question of whether or not poltergeists exist was now a lot harder to answer.

58. THE SEAFORD POLTERGEIST

In 1958, a series of strange events was reported by James M. Herrmann and his family in their home. The case was investigated by American parapsychologists Joseph Gaither Pratt and William G. Roll.

Roll is noted for his research into alleged poltergeist activity and for coining the term 'recurrent spontaneous psychokinesis' to explain it. In the case of the Seaford home in Long Island, New York, he believed that the events were unconsciously triggered by the Herrmanns' twelve-year-old son, James Jr. However, sceptics who have re-examined the case since have labelled Roll credulous in his belief in PK and suggested that James Jr was in fact the conscious or deliberate cause of the so-called poltergeist activity.

The activity began on 3 February 1958, when James Herrmann came home from work to find his family acting very strangely. He thought they had lost their minds. His wife, Lucille, told him that she and their teenage children, James and Lucy, were going about their normal routines after school when they heard popping sounds all around them. They investigated and found numerous bottles of common household products mysteriously uncapped in different rooms of the house. Ominously, there was also a bottle of holy water spilled across a bedroom dressing table.

Herrmann told his family to stay calm; there was probably a rational explanation. But five days later, when the family were eating a meal together, the popping sounds happened again. This time Herrmann was home and able to investigate himself. He discovered open and upended bottles in several rooms. He called in the police, and the officer who was dispatched to investigate also heard the weird popping noises and witnessed even more open bottles with their contents strewn across the floor. The officer could not explain what was going on, and later investigations by other officers also failed to draw any conclusions.

It wasn't long before the media found out and the story became public. A Catholic priest was invited into the house on 17 February to bless it, but this did absolutely nothing to calm things down. Many, including Herrmann himself, suspected it was caused by the teenage pranks of his children, but when a cousin of his visited the house and witnessed the popping with the teens sat opposite and in clear view, he changed his mind. Lucille even described the noise of rumbles throughout the house as so loud, it sounded 'like the walls were caving in'. Concerned for the safety of his family, Herrmann moved them all out temporarily.

On returning to the house, any hope that the popping and mess would have ceased was dashed as the ordeal resumed. This time heavier items were inexplicably pushed over. It was at this point that the Herrmann family was approached by Dr J. B. Rhine, director of Duke University's parapsychology laboratory. Rhine suggested that the energetic presence of two hormonal teenagers could be a conduit for PK to occur or potentially for a poltergeist to attach itself to.

Shortly after the Duke University scientists had arrived to investigate in earnest, as if by magic the mysterious popping noises stopped. There has still been no entirely convincing explanation for the seventy or so paranormal events that were experienced and recorded by the Herrmann family from 3 February to 10 March 1958. Whatever the explanation, the Seaford poltergeist case has continued to capture the imagination over the decades, with the 1982 Steven Spielberg horror movie *Poltergeist*, which is based on the events, ensuring its place in the paranormal hall of fame.

59. THE PONTEFRACT POLTERGEIST

The property at 30 East Drive is an unassuming semi-detached, three-bedroom family house on the Chequerfield Estate in Pontefract, Wales. It appears perfectly normal and everyday. But appearances can be deceptive, as some experts believe it to be one of the most haunted properties in the United Kingdom.

Reports of unexplained disturbances at the house began in 1966 and were featured in national newspapers when the Pritchard family, who were living there at the time, decided to go public about them. The Pritchard family consisted of wife and husband

Jean and Joe and their two teenage children, Diane and Philip. The first supernatural experience happened to Philip when both he and his grandmother noticed white dust falling from thin air at about head height with no apparent explanation. Other uncanny things happened after that, including doors shutting by themselves, lights inexplicably switching on and off, and sludgy green liquid coming out of the taps. Puddles of water also started appearing on the kitchen floor, and any attempt to dry them failed. When the council visited to investigate the water problem, no cause could be found.

Soon the disturbances upgraded to objects mysteriously flying through the air, a grandfather clock falling down the stairs and photographs being cut apart. Things escalated to dangerous places when Diane claimed an invisible hand had grabbed her by the hair and pulled her kicking and screaming from the bottom of the stairs to the top. Angry red choking marks appeared around her throat.

If the story sounds familiar, it may be because the events that took place at 30 East Drive were dramatized in a move called *When the Lights Went Out*. Artistic licence was taken with the film to make it entertaining to watch, but it has been praised for being a realistic depiction of life in a British council house in the 1960s and is true to the contemporary reports.

At the time, the house got unprecedented media coverage, ensuring it remains a mecca for paranormal investigators and TV shows and for psychics to visit and hold seances. Since the Pritchards left the house, it has remained empty and has become a popular venue for ghost hunts and tours. The house remains frozen in its 1970s era, complete with faded pictures of the Osmonds on the wall. Several theories for the paranormal activity have been put forward.

One of those is that there is a well directly under the house and the location of the house is directly across the street from where the town gallows once stood, suggesting that the traumatic energy associated with that gallows imprinted itself onto the house. Mediums at the time suggested that a sixteenth-century monk was hanged there for the murder of a young girl and his body later thrown down the well. Some believe that ever since, the monk's ghost has been trapped there in torment, and there have been reports of an apparition dressed in long black robes. The Pritchards named this monk Fred, or the Black Monk of Pontefract.

This theory has been challenged, with some saying the well, or even an underground stream or brook, never ran through the site of the house, as no sign of them has been found underground or on ancient maps. Psychics have also suggested that the house was haunted by the monk's victim, a little girl who responds to the name of Emma. Unlike the monk, who has a nasty energy, her energy is playful. Other mediums have linked the paranormal activity to the nearby site of the Battle of Chequerfield and the residual energy of brutal and bloody battle during the English Civil War lingering on in the house.

The poltergeist activity has been directly linked by some to the conscious or unconscious actions of the Pritchard children, with or without the knowledge of their parents. However, others are committed to the belief that an evil, sinister entity still resides at 30 East Drive.

60. THE ROSENHEIM POLTERGEIST

The Rosenheim Poltergeist is the name given to a well-documented poltergeist case that happened in 1967 in the southern Bavarian town of Rosenheim.

It started in the law office of Sigmund Adam when staff heard loud banging noises and endured a series of electrical malfunctions. Telephones stopped and then started working again for no reason, and photocopiers appeared to have a life of their own. In addition, pictures started to rotate and telephone numbers were dialled by invisible means. Things took an even more bizarre turn when Sigmund's office was charged for local calls made to the talking clock. The telephone company charged for six calls per minute, which was impossible given the time it would take to dial the number and the other end to pick up and respond. The telephone company could not explain how this was possible either.

Investigators were called in and were completely mystified. Electricians were equally nonplussed. One theory suggested by German parapsychologist Hans Bender from the Freiburg Institute of Paranormal Research was that the electrical disturbances in particular were caused by the telepathic powers of the firm's nineteen-year-old secretary, Annemarie Schaberl. He noted that the disturbances only occurred when Annemarie was present and that when she walked down the hallway, light bulbs spontaneously exploded. It was suggested the unexplained telephone dialling was caused by 'intelligently controlled forces that have a tendency to evade investigation'. Bender believed this was an open and shut case of a 'typical poltergeist' being caused by the unconscious or conscious emotional tension of the human agent, Annemarie, being 'converted into psychokinesis'. He argued that she disliked and felt frustrated by her job and was also suffering from the acute stress of a dysfunctional relationship.

Bender's PK conclusion has been strongly criticized for not being detailed enough and for avoiding other logical explanations. However, it is worth pointing out that the alleged poltergeist disturbance did stop when Annemarie left the law firm.

In 1970, German weekly newspaper *Die Zeit* published a feature based on a book entitled *False Spirits, Real Swindlers*. Both feature and book suggested that the claims made by Adam were entirely fraudulent and that trickery, such as nylon threads attached to office fixtures to make them appear to move on their own, was behind it all. This sounds entirely plausible – with the exception of there being no clear motive for such elaborate trickery. Why would anyone want to do business with a haunted law office? Sigmund unsuccessfully filed a legal injunction to stop publication of the book.

A few years later, John Taylor, a noted British physicist and author who believed paranormal phenomena typically had a naturalistic explanation, also investigated the case. Taylor reflected deeply on the case and declared that the alleged poltergeist activity at the Rosenheim law firm was very likely to be a combination of 'expectation, hallucination and trickery'. Despite this, the case of the Rosenheim poltergeist remains hotly debated, unexplained and unsolved.

61. THE AMITYVILLE POLTERGEIST

Continuing the trend of the majority of poltergeist activity being attributed to simple fraud, now we turn to one of the most famous and heavily reported cases of alleged poltergeist activity in the world to date: the Amityville Poltergeist.

The property at 112 Ocean Avenue in Amityville, New York, no longer exists. There is a good reason the house's former identity is masked: to deter the stream of visitors curious to see the house of evil for themselves. It all began in 1974, when twenty-three-year-old Ronnie DeFeo chillingly shot and murdered his mother, father and four siblings while they were all living in the house.

Initially Ronnie denied he was the murderer and said it was a mob killing. To add to the confusion, none of the neighbours reported hearing gunshots that night, even though the family had been shot by a rifle with no silencer. They did report hearing the family dog barking wildly at the time, though. Eventually the police became convinced he was responsible and he confessed. However, he also said he had heard their voices plotting against him in his head and pleaded insanity. As a result of this plea, he was incarcerated for the rest of his life. He died in 2021, and right up until his death, he continued to fabricate different versions of events that day, including stories suggesting that his parents had been responsible.

George and Kathleen Lutz and their three children from Kathy's previous marriage – Daniel, aged nine; Christopher, aged seven; and Melissa (Missy), aged five – moved into the house about a year after the murders and the trial. The house was placed on the market at a bargain price because of its bloody past. The Lutzes said they did not know what had happened there when they first purchased it, and a lot of the furniture and items used by the murdered family were still in place when they moved in.

In a matter of weeks, scary things resembling poltergeist activity started happening in the house. Doors were flung open and slammed shut of their own accord, furniture moved by itself, and swarms of flies and oozing black slime mysteriously appeared. Shapes that resembled grotesque faces appeared on the walls, and constant rapping sounds were heard. It was not long before the family discovered the truth about the house's past and decided to ask a priest to bless the property in the hope of exorcising the resident evil. The priest duly blessed each room but said he sensed the presence of a male in the house and heard a harsh and abrupt voice telling him to 'get out'. The priest also allegedly witnessed Kathy levitating and crucifixes turning upside down.

The day after his visit to the house, the priest fell sick with a severe fever and developed stigmata-like blisters on his hands. The Lutzes only lasted about a month in the house until it became too frightening and dangerous for them to live there. They felt they had no choice but to leave immediately. They did not even wait to take any belongings with them and arranged for a moving service to pack everything up for them. They ended up selling their story to a writer called Jay Anson, who turned it into a 1977 bestselling book, *The Amityville Horror: A True Story*. The book sold over 6 million copies. It was not long before film rights were sold too, and it became the top grossing film of 1979.

Due to the popularity of both book and film, 112 Ocean Avenue was thought for a long time to rank among the most haunted places in the world. Daniel was nine years old at the time of the haunting, and he later revealed that he hated his stepfather George with a passion, making him a likely human agent for the poltergeist hypothesis. However, the tale is a real mishmash of classic haunting, poltergeist and demonic attack. And this blurring of boundaries – plus the likelihood of fraud and the explanation being related to the living rather than the dead or undead – is one of many reasons serious doubt has been cast on the truth of this story.

When the Lutzes moved out, the house became quiet. The next owners, Jim and Barbara Cromarty, said they experienced nothing paranormal. However, they grew so annoyed with tourists flocking to the house that they sued the Lutzes and their publishing house,

Prentice Hall. They won a settlement for an undisclosed amount, with the judge ruling that 'the evidence shows fairly clearly that the Lutzes during the entire period were considering and acting with the thought of getting a book published'.

Although in its day the case was taken very seriously by leading ghost hunter Hans Holzer, and some continue to believe a poltergeist was at work, it is largely considered a hoax by the modern paranormal community. Still, it is always possible a demonic entity may have attacked the Lutzes or that the unhappy Lutz children were unconsciously or consciously causing disturbances – and the priest's story is certainly worth considering further as an independent witness outside the family. The whole truth may never be known.

62. THE AMHERST POLTERGEIST

The Amherst haunting – also known as the Great Amherst Mystery – is a tale of alleged poltergeist activity that took place in a small two-room cottage in Amherst, Nova Scotia, way back in 1878. It focused on a young woman called Esther Coz, who lived there with her extended family.

Nineteen-year-old Esther had been threatened with attempted rape at gunpoint by a family friend, and one night soon afterwards, she understandably felt anxious, so, craving time alone, she went to bed early. In the middle of the night she sat bolt upright and started screaming that she was dying. It is said that 'her eyes were bloodshot, her hair stood on end and her body puffed up twice its normal size'. As she screamed, thunderous bangs could be heard coming from beneath her bed. Her sheets were ripped off and tossed into the corner of the room.

Esther's family went to fetch the local doctor. When the good doctor arrived to administer sedatives, he witnessed Esther's screaming seizure as well as furniture moving by itself and the words 'Esther Coz you are mine to kill' a foot tall, being scratched as if by invisible claws across the wall.

The disturbances continued for several months afterwards. Unexplained fires sprang up out of nowhere on Esther's bed. Eventually, enough damage had been done to the property and it was decided that Esther had to leave. She went to stay with a selection of different people, but it seems she took her troubles with her. The barn of a man called Arthur Davison, who she briefly went to work for, was mysteriously set on fire, and Esther was charged with arson. She was convicted and sent to jail for four months, though she only served one.

After she left jail, there were only brief episodes of disturbances, and over time they stopped completely. Esther went on to marry twice and died in 1912 at the age of fifty-two.

During her lifetime the story of Esther Coz became well known in Amherst, and she had a series of visitors who allegedly witnessed the weird events happening around her. She drew the attention of an actor called Walter Hubbell, who had a fascination with psychic matters. He kept a diary of events and published a book about it in 1879. The problem with the book is that it asserts all the events were corroborated by witnesses, but no evidence of this has been found. This has led some to the conclusion that the case was a hoax engineered by Hubbell, who took advantage of vulnerable Esther – she appears to have accompanied him on a speaking tour to promote the book.

The mysterious case of Esther Coz remains unsolved. Some have suggested electricity was the catalyst. Electricity was entirely new at the time and was regarded with great suspicion, as people did not really understand how something invisible worked and behaved. Another explanation for the spontaneous fires is that they were caused by lightning bolts and the banging noises in Esther's bedroom were accompanying thunderclaps.

Those who subscribe to the PK hypothesis as an explanation for poltergeist attacks believe Esther was the unconscious human agent. Repressed anxiety following her threatened rape, and the cramped and stressful conditions she and her family endured in the small cottage may have caused the phenomena. There has also been speculation that she may have suffered from split personality disorder, and Walter D. Prince of the American Society for Psychical Research is quoted as saying, 'She herself, or rather part of her, played "poltergeist".'

63. THE JABOTICABAL POLTERGEIST

The invisible attacks that took place in Jaboticabal, around 200 miles north of São Paulo in Brazil, are a potent reminder of the potential deadly consequences whenever alleged poltergeist incidents are reported.

In December 1965, a respected Catholic family reported bricks inexplicably falling inside their home. At first they thought it must either be a problem with construction or that someone was throwing the bricks from outside. When both explanations were ruled out, a local priest was called in to perform an exorcism. It didn't help, and the bricks kept on appearing out of nowhere.

The family turned to their neighbour, João Volpe, a man known for his expertise in psychic matters. He was convinced that the cause of the disturbance was eleven-year-old Maria Jose Ferreira. Volpe believed this to be a classic case of poltergeist activity and that Maria was a natural medium who could talk to spirits, so, with her parents' consent, he invited Maria to stay at his home to see if the phenomena continued. After a few days of peace, the bricks started raining down again whenever Maria was present. Volpe recorded at least 300 falling stones. Eggs also began to mysteriously appear and disappear, as did sweets, cups and glasses. There were also instances of furniture moving all by itself and pictures falling off walls.

Around five or so weeks after the first brick falling, Maria was attacked by needles, some of which embedded themselves deep into her skin. On 14 March 1966, Maria's clothes spontaneously caught fire when she was at school and a fire broke out on the same day in Volpe's bedroom, burning Volpe.

After many months of disturbances, Volpe sought the advice of a mentor. He took Maria to see Brazil's most famous medium at the time, Chico Xavier. The medium recklessly announced that spirits had told him Maria was a bad witch and in a former life she had practised black magic and deliberately caused the suffering and deaths of many people. Now the spirits of her enemies were seeking their revenge on her spirit in this life. Maria was 'treated' by blessings and group prayer, and after that the disturbances did seem to subside, with only the odd vegetable- and fruit-throwing incident.

Maria returned to live with her mother when she was thirteen. Tragically, she was found dead in 1970 at the tender age of sixteen, having consumed a soft drink laced with pesticide. Perhaps she could endure her life no longer. Perhaps she was murdered. Or perhaps an invisible entity had forced her to drink her poison.

After her death, the disturbances stopped entirely. Although the likely cause of her death seems to be psychological abuse inflicted on a young girl by misinformed and unqualified spiritual 'experts', the mystery of the poltergeist activity and why, who or what exactly led young Maria to tragically take her own life remains unsolved.

64. THE SAUCHIE POLTERGEIST

Virginia Campbell was eleven years old and the youngest of seven children to Irish parents James and Annie Campbell. The family had been raised in County Donegal, but in the autumn of 1960, Virginia and her mother relocated to Sauchie in Scotland. They moved in to a house in Park Crescent that belonged to Virginia's brother, Thomas, who already lived in Sauchie with his wife Isabella and their young daughter Margaret and son Derek.

While her mother went to work at a local boarding house, Virginia was left to live with her uncle's family and share a bedroom with her younger cousin Margaret. She was enrolled in a local school, where her teacher noticed that she was bright and polite but that she did have problems making friends. She was initially very lonely and struggled to adjust to her new life.

The night of 22 November 1960 was the first date of disturbances in the Campbell home. A 'thunking' sound rather like a ball bouncing on the wall was heard in the girls' bedroom and the noise began to follow them around the house, only stopping when Virginia was asleep. The next day, a sideboard moved by itself and scratching sounds were heard along with the thunking. The Campbells grew concerned and contacted a local pastor from the Church of England, Reverend Lund.

Rev. Lund visited the house and, along with the family doctor, witnessed the unusual happenings. At her school, Virginia's teacher said she saw the girl's desk levitate. On 1 December, the doctor and the reverend set up a video camera and recorded weird sounds when Virginia went into a trance. At 11 p.m. that same day, an unsuccessful religious intervention was performed, with the banging sound continuing throughout.

On 2 December, the story hit the press and the house swiftly became notorious in Sauchie. Concerned for Virginia's wellbeing, the doctor suddenly announced that she was cured. His bold move appears to have worked, as the phenomena almost immediately began to diminish, apart from the odd incident. By March the following year, peace of mind had returned to Virginia and to Sauchie.

British mathematician and parapsychologist Alan Robert George Owen, noted for his championing of the PK explanation for poltergeist phenomena, investigated the case and interviewed the Campbells. He concluded that they were a well-adjusted, stable family and there was no clear trigger. As well as ruling out natural explanations such as draughts and trickery on the part of Virginia and the other children, he also ruled out paranormal entities, as nobody sensed an evil presence. Even Virginia did not appear anxious about the activity happening around her.

The conclusion Owen drew was that this was a clear-cut case of PK on the part of Virginia. She was going through puberty when the activity occurred, and this may have generated enough unconscious energy to create poltergeist forces. These forces were likely to have been triggered by self-consciousness about the changes her body was going through, as well as missing her father and her dog and taking time to get used to a new setting.

Owen's PK theory seems to dominate literature concerning the Sauchie poltergeist, but the case remains unsolved and stands out because so many people witnessed the paranormal incidents and were willing to go on record about them. It is certainly a remarkable case, but what is refreshing here is that the adults involved had the good sense to stop intrusive investigations. The doctor's timely decision to declare Virginia 'cured' was deeply empathetic to her plight. It probably prevented her and her family from being exploited and harassed by the media and saved her from misinformed attempts at 'diagnosis' or 'cures', which may in time have proved deeply damaging or even deadly.

65. THE BATTERSEA POLTERGEIST

The Battersea poltergeist is a case of suspected paranormal activity that began in January 1956 with the mysterious appearance of a silver key on the pillow of fifteen-year-old Shirley Hitchings. Shirley lived in a Victorian house in Wycliffe Road, Battersea, south-west London with her mother Kitty and her dad Wally, a London Underground driver, as well as her Irish grandmother Ethel and her adopted brother John.

Shirley had never seen the key before and neither had anyone in her family. It did not fit any locks in her room or the house. That night, as the family were preparing to go to sleep, they were terrified by loud thumping and banging sounds, as well as claw-like scratching from inside the furniture and lights switching on and off by themselves. Neighbours heard the noise too, as this was typically a quiet area, and it was so loud that some of them went round to the house to complain. Decades later, Shirley recalled how traumatizing the knocking was and how she clung to her father and begged him to make the noises stop.

The noises and the terror didn't stop from that point. In fact, they returned and intensified night after night for the next twelve years, making this poltergeist case stand out for its frightening longevity. There were no further gifts left on Shirley's pillow – the silver key vanished without a trace – but she did report being dragged from her bed by an invisible force that made her levitate. At one point an independent reporter named Joyce Lewis slept overnight in Shirley's room and witnessed her being clawed and pulled out of bed in a truly terrifying encounter. Messages were scrawled on the walls, objects were thrown and small fires erupted in the house. Not surprisingly, the strange events became a local and then a national news story and were even at one point mentioned in Parliament. The family would later give the force a name – Donald, named after Disney's Donald Duck.

The Battersea poltergeist case remains unexplained to this day. A hugely popular BBC Sounds podcast which began in 2021 attempted to solve the mystery of whether it was a hoax or a paranormal event. The podcast drew inspiration from the documents of ghost hunter Harold Chibbett, known affectionately as Chib by the family. Chibbett investigated the case in the 1950s and devoted the rest of his life to it, as he believed it could definitively prove there was life after death. Chibbett interviewed many witnesses, as well as Shirley and her family, and the podcast producer Danny Robins, who immersed himself in the case for several years to create the podcast, believes this case may be the closest there is to proof that ghosts exist.

Chib suggested to the family that they were dealing with a poltergeist – not a poltergeist in the sense that it was unconscious PK on the part of Shirley, but instead an external force or entity that had latched itself onto her. The family believed Chib and arranged for Shirley to be exorcised at the home of a medium called Harry Hanks. However, the exorcism never happened, because someone tipped off the police about potential 'witchcraft and black magic'. This led to the haunting being discussed in the House of Commons, with Hanks's MP asking the police to apologize to the medium for the intrusion into what was a private matter.

Donald the poltergeist continued to haunt the house, leaving a frenzy of messages scrawled on the walls. Chib decided to leave a pen and paper in the family's front room – the only room in the house with a lock – and he took the key home with him. Over time this room became known as 'Donald's room', and Chib's files contain thousands of notes, many of which can be viewed online. Most are impossible to read, but some, such as 'Shirley, I come', are chillingly clear. At times the messages blur into French.

The French is significant, as at one point 'Donald' claimed to be the 'lost dauphin' of Louis Charles and Marie Antoinette, once heir to the French throne. The fate of the ten-year-old prince remains unknown, and notes from Donald appear to contain details few would have known but which can be verified, such as the names of the boy's bodyguards.

Things took an even darker turn from March 1956, when Donald became threatening and menacingly spoke to Ethel, Shirley's grandmother, in her mother's voice. A few days after that unsettling incident, Ethel died of a stroke.

The activity wasn't confined to the home in Battersea either, and it seemed to follow Shirley. She was fired from her job as a seamstress in Selfridges when scissors went missing and she was believed to be the thief; even today Shirley maintains it was Donald playing pranks. Strange things continued to happen when in 1964 the family moved to another house in nearby Latchmere Road. Shirley said that the poltergeist ruined her teenage years, making it impossible for her to have a normal life and relationships.

Despite this, both Shirley and her family somehow adjusted to the presence of Donald in their lives. A goodbye message to Shirley was found in 1968 when she was living in West Sussex with her husband, and Donald never returned after that. Although Shirley was happy, her mother was sad. She said she began to regard Donald as her invisible son.

The Battersea poltergeist case is well documented and an unusually large number of witnesses, including the police, appear to verify it. However, it is important to point out that the power of suggestion may have been at work here, and a growing number of paranormal experts believe that all cases of poltergeist activity are in some way or another hoaxes. This could be the case here, and you certainly can't rule out that the intriguing messages from Donald were scribbled by Chib in his desire to prove the afterlife is real, or by Shirley or a member of her family.

Perhaps the most arresting aspect of this case, however, is the human agent herself – Shirley. When Robins interviewed her for his podcast, she came across to both him and his millions of listeners as honest, sincere and normal. And it is certainly true that while some of the events can be explained by natural causes or trickery, there are a lot that can't.

INHUMAN

'The demons are innumerable, appear at the most inconvenient times, and create panic and terror. But I have learnt that if I can master the negative forces and harness them to my chariot, then they can work to my advantage.'

Ingmar Bergman

You may automatically think demons and other malevolent supernatural entities entirely define the term 'inhuman', but it can also reference any kind of haunting that is believed to be caused by what is non-human or which has never lived as a human. It can include angels, for example, as well as benevolent (or not) elemental or nature spirits with supernatural powers, such as fairies, elves and goblins. Animism is the belief that elemental energies or forces inhabit all living things, and it is a belief that predates all the major religions. Animals, objects and portals can also fall into this wildly eclectic category, as can orbs. An orb is a light anomaly that is captured on camera or video. It is not always round and can appear as a thread or a mist, but traditionally it is a spherical ball of light.

Demonic hauntings, however, are the most commonly reported and documented in this category, perhaps because they have the greatest potential to cause terror and real harm to those involved

– also because they have a habit of capturing the attention not just of the media and public but of many a horror writer and movie director. The huge popularity of horror books and movies, such as the trendsetting *The Exorcist* (1973), gives the impression that cases of demonic haunting and possession are far more common than they are, when in fact real-life cases are exceedingly rare.

Demons

Demonic hauntings can sometimes appear interchangeable with poltergeist hauntings in that there is a human victim or victims the activity clusters around. Whether this dark transformation is caused by an entity latching onto its victim or is the manifestation of conscious or unconscious psychological torment remains an open question for both poltergeist and demonic hauntings. Indeed, some entries in the previous category could have sat just as well in this category. But it is possible to identify certain characteristics specific to demonic hauntings.

First and foremost, the hallmark of demonic hauntings is absolute terror. There is nothing remotely playful or benign going on here, as is sometimes the case with poltergeist cases. Demons are believed to be entirely evil. Some believe they are dangerous non-human spirits or forces that have existed on earth since time began. Others suggest they may be fallen angels sent by the devil to plague and torment humans.

You may also come across contemporary reports of demons or ghosts that allegedly rape their victims at night. Victims of a succubus (female demon who attacks when a man is sleeping) or incubus (male demon whose nocturnal attentions are horrifying to women) report waking abruptly in the night to find that they cannot move, although they can still see, hear, feel and smell. There may be a feeling of a heavy weight on their chest and the sense of an evil presence violating them. Sceptics argue that this is more likely to be a medical disorder, such as indigestion or a particularly vivid nightmare or an anxiety attack caused by repressed tension and stress.

Chances are it may be due to sleep paralysis, a perfectly natural stage in falling asleep and waking when you begin to doze off but parts of your brain remain active. Lasting from a few seconds to a minute or two, this happens every night, but most of the time you are unaware of it.

Some occult experts believe demons pick their victims randomly, as they detest all humanity, but others believe they are attracted to people and places where there has been a tremendous amount of stress, depression, violence, anger and intensely negative emotional energy. Devil worship using a Ouija board, satanic rituals and witchcraft are also believed to summon demons from the depths. When demons manifest, their purpose is to inspire as much fear, chaos, hatred and negativity as possible in their chosen victims.

And it is not just people that can be possessed. If reports are to be believed, objects can be infected with negative forces too. This inhuman category also includes entries where it appears that some kind of dark energy has taken over an object. These objects can be ancient and valuable, but they can also be hauntingly everyday, like a mirror, a doll or even a photograph.

Signs of a potential case of demonic haunting also include religious objects such as crosses being damaged or turned around. It is thought religious objects are a threat to them. The unexplained stench of sulphur or other rotten-smelling odours is another symptom, as is household pets reacting strangely. Many people believe animals can see what humans cannot. There are also menacing, inhuman sounds with no explainable source, such as scratching, howling, hellish moaning, banging and knocking. Last but by no means least, the victim or victims will experience a constant feeling of dread, as well as physical symptoms such as mysterious bruises and scratches and feelings of nausea and overwhelming fatigue. It is as if the demon is quite literally draining the life out of them.

In some cases, the victim will become so withdrawn and depressed, and experience such a change in personality after a demonic presence reveals itself in their home, that those around them and medical professionals may question their sanity. It is as if they are no longer themselves and are entirely possessed by the demonic presence. They have totally succumbed to the demon's physical, mental and emotional attack. And when this happens, the explanation is, rightly or wrongly, often attributed to some form of mental illness. And when the situation becomes intolerable, this is often when concerned loved ones in their desperation may consider an exorcism as the only remedy.

Exorcism

Exorcism is the ritual process by which an evil spirit or demon is driven out of a human host, object or place. It comes from the Greek word *exorkizein*, meaning 'bind by oath', and is the invoking of a higher power to make a spirit act in a certain way. It is typically performed by trained religious officials or occult experts. Rites range from simple prayer to specific techniques such as fasting and blessing with holy water. Exorcisms in the Catholic Church date back to medieval times, with priests performing rituals to expel demons from their human victims.

Exorcism rituals can also be found in shamanic cultures, as well as in Hinduism, Buddhism, Islam and Judaism. In China, evil spirits are exorcised from places by Taoist priests in a complex ritual involving mystical signs and scrolls. Within Christianity, the Roman Catholic Church today still offers a formal rite of exorcism, the *Rituale Romanun*, which dates back to 1614. The Pope can instruct priests to send a potential case of possession to a qualified exorcist if they believe there is 'genuine spiritual disturbance'. Thankfully, priests are also instructed to consult a medical doctor at the same time. The criteria for diagnosis is very strict, and the exorcising priest must have 'moral certainty'. In order to qualify as a candidate for exorcism, the victim must display certain symptoms, including superhuman strength, levitation and speaking in tongues (*glossolalia*).

Although the practice was rare by the 1970s, the huge popularity of movies like *The Exorcist* dramatically revived interest. From 2005 onwards, the Vatican has run an annual exorcism course entitled 'Exorcism and the Prayer of Liberation', with no shortage of eager participants. Priests travel from all over the world to attend and learn how to expel potential demons. Their expertise is apparently much in demand, with hundreds of thousands of people each year requesting exorcisms. The most serious concerns involving exorcisms, whether conducted by a qualified priest or not, is that the safety of the person being exorcised can so easily be overlooked. There may also be accompanying health and psychological issues that require the expertise of a trained doctor or psychiatrist, not an 'exorcist'.

Some paranormal psychologists suggest that possessing spirits are not evil but simply confused and trying to interact with the world through a living person. This can cause mental problems in the human agent, and in his controversial book *Thirty Years Among the Dead* (1924), one prominent expert, Carl Wickland, recommended using mild electric shock treatment to encourage the spirits to leave the body. This view that possession is due to possessing spirits has supporters, among them psychiatrist Dr Ralph Allison, who wrote in his book *Minds in Many Places* (1980) that his patients exhibited signs of demonic possession and needed exorcism as well as conventional treatment.

Handle with care

Sadly, some cases of demonic possession have resulted in the death of the victim, underlining the vital importance of treating any case where there is talk of an allegedly demonic entity with the utmost seriousness and for doctors and mental health professionals to be involved from the outset.

Sceptics argue that demonic attacks are either psychiatric disorders or the products of an overactive imagination. They may also be cases of superstitious beliefs getting out of hand and/or simple fraud. These rational explanations may certainly be true in some cases, but as this section will show you, it is hard to explain away all potential cases of demonic haunting in this way.

Note: A brief note here about the difference between a demon and a vampire. There is a lot of confusion between the two. Both are undead spirits associated with darkness, death and destruction, but the simple difference is that vampires, unlike demons, are believed to require human blood to survive, suggesting that they are both living and dead. This book could have included many alleged vampire sightings – as well as references to reports of zombies (flesh-devouring undead) and werewolves (wolf people), not to mention UFOs and aliens – as all are clearly paranormal and out of this world, but to do so might stray too far from the ghostly remit of this book.

Portal hauntings

Slightly less menacing in nature, but matching the controversy and confusion surrounding demonic possession, are portal hauntings. They are not as well understood or investigated as other types of hauntings, but the general consensus among paranormal investigators is that they are a kind of 'door' from this world to the afterlife or an alternative reality. And sometimes ghosts of the dead and inhuman entities can slip right through into our world.

Portal hauntings, if they exist, could explain why some locations appear to attract reports of paranormal and/or supernatural activity. They may also 'explain' stories of alleged time travel into the past or future, or entry to another reality or parallel universe, as well as doppelgänger stories.

Theories put forward for portals include the existence of magnetic ley or energy lines beneath the earth's surface – when these ley lines cross or intersect, strange things can happen, such as hauntings and apparitions but also unexplained lights or orbs and shadowy creatures or figures. These ley lines can allegedly be sensed by psychics, dowsers (someone who uses a diving rod typically to find underground water) or specialist ghost-hunting equipment. Empathetic and highly sensitive people may also tune in to them. There is also a school of occult thought which believes these portals can be unlocked by dark or satanic rituals.

The term 'ley line' was proposed by a man called Alfred Watkins in 1925. It is derived from the Saxon word which means a 'woodland clearing'. Watkins examined prehistoric maps of England and noticed certain alignments between ancient sacred sites such as churches and graveyards, as well as places of mystical significance, like Stonehenge. It is thought that a portal can be opened or reactivated whenever there is intense trauma or a building is renovated or even when there is great humidity or when all these factors synergize.

Portal hauntings are not limited to natural and sacred sites, however. Crossover points can occur anywhere at any time, even in ordinary houses or public areas. Sometimes the inhuman negative entities that can enter through them may be awakened by satanic rituals, but it is also thought that intense emotion and trauma can activate them and they can also open up spontaneously.

Still right out there

A number of out-of-this-world theories exist to open your mind to the idea that a variety of inhuman hauntings can and do happen. But it is important to remind yourself that so much more research needs to be done and, to date, all these strange theories remain just that – theories.

66. ROBERT

It is only fitting that the first entry number for this Inhuman category is 66 – traditionally, repeating sixes are widely recognized as a symbol of the Antichrist, the devil or what is diabolic. And what better way to begin than with perhaps the most frightening doll in the world, the Robert doll.

Robert the doll first appears in the year 1904 at 534 Eaton Street in Key West, Florida, when he was given to Robert Eugene Otto, also known by his family nickname Gene, as a birthday present from his grandfather, who had recently bought the doll on a trip to Germany. Some versions claim that a young girl of 'Bahamian descent' gave Otto the doll as a gift – or as a curse for some kind of wrongdoing. Either way, Steiff historians have suggested the figure was never intended to be a toy but, with his nub of a nose and pinholes for nostrils, black beady eyes and pockmarked skin, was rather a mannequin for shop window displays.

The grandfather dressed the toddler-sized straw doll in one of Gene's favourite sailor suits and it soon became Gene's favourite toy. The little boy would take the doll everywhere with him and affectionately named it Robert after himself.

As imaginative children often do, Gene loved to talk to his favourite toy as if it were real. When they passed his bedroom, his parents and their servants would often hear him talking in his own voice before replying in an entirely different voice for his doll. However, things took a sinister turn when Gene started to have nightmares, waking up screaming in the night to find Robert sitting at the end of his bed. When his parents came to his bedroom, they found furniture overturned and toys scattered everywhere. A visibly terrified Gene insisted it was Robert who had created the mayhem.

Soon, toys started to be broken more frequently and objects mysteriously moved around the house. Again, Gene said that 'Robert did it'. His parents did not believe him, but some of their servants reported hearing giggling and footsteps on the stairs and in his bedroom when it was empty. Passers-by outside the house also reported seeing the doll moving in the room or staring out of the window. When Gene left home to study art, Robert was stored away in the attic for several years.

In 1930, Gene married Annette Parker and was establishing his career as an 'eccentric' artist. After his parents died, Gene moved back into his childhood Florida home with Annette. He rescued Robert from the attic, and despite Annette's reluctance he gave it pride of place in his art studio, which had previously been his second-floor turret playroom. There are several accounts of what happened in that house before Gene died in 1974 and Annette in 1976. Some say Robert's antics drove Annette insane, others that when Gene died, Robert was inexplicably found in the room.

For the next two decades, Robert the doll remained at the house after it was sold. Today, the property has become a guest house and it is possible to stay in the old turret room that Robert stared out of, but the doll itself is now placed in a glass box fitted with alarms and can be viewed at the Fort East Martello Museum. The careworn doll sits there still to this day wearing the faded sailor's outfit. With a hint of a smirk he holds a toy in his hands: a dog with an overly long tongue and eyes that pop.

Over the years many who have visited Robert in his glass cage have reported feelings of dread. Some have even claimed to see the doll's face and limbs move by themselves, his expression changing in the corners of their eyes, and, more terrifying still, have heard the doll giggle when their backs are turned. Coincidentally or not, people who have come into contact with Robert or visited him have found themselves showered with misfortune and bad luck afterwards, such as car accidents, illness, job loss and divorce. It is said that this is because when they were in his presence, they did not show him enough respect or did not politely ask his permission before taking his photograph.

This all sounds very far-fetched indeed. But a glance at the number of letters posted on the walls beside Robert's glass case, entreating the doll's forgiveness for their tardiness or begging him to remove his curse, and the pacifying gifts and sweets visitors leave him perhaps suggest otherwise. And if you think this story is a gift for a horror writer and director, you are right. A popular horror franchise based on the story of Robert the doll, entitled *Robert*, was released in 2015, with four sequels following in the years after: *The Curse of Robert the Doll*; *The Toymaker*; *The Revenge of Robert the Doll*; and *Robert Reborn*.

67. ANNABELLE

If dolls can have siblings, Robert the doll's terrifying twin sister would undoubtedly be Annabelle, another allegedly cursed doll.

The Raggedy Ann doll – who would later become known simply as Annabelle – was one of the most popular items in the Warrens' Occult Museum in Monroe, Connecticut, formerly owned and run by American paranormal investigators Ed and Lorraine Warren. It appears to have been a gift to a nursing student called Donna in 1970, but almost immediately Donna and her roommate noticed that the doll seemed to inexplicably change positions and move about the room. The two women also began to find notes reading 'Help me' on parchment paper around the house. They asked a psychic for advice, and the psychic determined the doll was possessed by the spirit of a little girl called Annabelle Higgins. The girl had died for unknown reasons and her spirit simply wanted to be cared for and loved.

Not long after the intervention of the psychic, the doll allegedly terrorized one of Donna's friends – led on a goose chase round the house following mysterious rustling noises, he found Annabelle face down on the floor and suddenly felt a searing pain in his chest, looking down to find bloody claw marks had been etched into his skin. Donna contacted a priest for advice this time. It was the priest who sought the help of the Warrens, and it was the Warrens who determined that this was not a benign spirit inhabiting the doll but a demonic one in search of a human host. They decided the doll was too dangerous to live with Donna, so they took it home with them.

Annabelle was locked safely away in a glass and wood case in the Warrens' now-closed occult museum. The Warrens began to document stories about the doll. They came to the conclusion that anyone who came into contact with her – and especially anyone who disrespected the doll – was unwittingly inviting sadness and bad luck into their lives. Strange and often unfortunate events, including fatal accidents, were more likely to occur afterwards too. On one occasion, a visitor who laughed at the doll and knocked on her case was killed in a motorbike accident on his way home.

Sceptics suggest that the story of Annabelle is the result of the merging of paranormal folklore, superstition and the overactive imagination of horror movie writers and directors, as well as potentially the Warrens themselves. It is also interesting to note that the opening of the Warrens' occult museum dovetailed with the release of *The Conjuring*, the first film in what would become the highest-grossing horror movie franchise to date, in which the Warrens were portrayed in lead roles. Indeed, the Warrens' description of the doll served as inspiration for the doll character of the same name depicted in *Annabelle*, *Annabelle: Creation* and *Annabelle Comes Home*.

As a result, it is hard to separate the truth about Annabelle from the sensational movie portrayal, especially as all the evidence for the doll being demonically possessed is anecdotal or gathered by the Warrens, who are no longer with us. Also, for trademark reasons and to make the doll look more frightening than it actually is in real life, the likeness of the Raggedy Ann doll in the movies does not bear many similarities to the original Annabelle. Yet still the notion of a demon possessing a simple rag doll remains a chilling reminder that evil can lurk in the most innocent places.

68. THE DYBBUK BOX

The Hebrew word *dybbuk* originates from a word that means 'to cleave' or 'to cling'. According to Jewish lore, a *dybbuk* is a disembodied malignant spirit that can enter a person's body and cling tightly to it. Some believe *dybbuks* are the souls of people who have not been buried properly and so they become demons.

The Kabbalah, a set of sacred Jewish mystical teachings, has instructions for how to exorcise a *dybbuk*, which is thought to exit the body via the small toe and leave a bloody mark there on departure. In early lore, the *dybbuk* was only believed to inhabit the bodies of people who were sick, and there are references to the possession and exorcism of *dybbuk* spirits in the Old Testament. However, by the early sixteenth century many Jews believed a *dybbuk* could not enter an innocent body but only inhabit the body of a sinner.

Superstition has it that a *dybbuk* can be trapped inside a box, and that box can contain the evil it wants to unleash unless the box is opened. One such box exists today and is believed by some to be the most haunted object in the world. Originally designed to store wine bottles, when people came into contact with the box they began to report strange feelings and smells. The original owner believed that the box contained an evil spirit trapped there during the Holocaust.

It all began in 2003 when Kevin Mannis, an antiques dealer from Oregon, US, placed the box for sale on eBay. He said he had bought it at an auction following the death of a 103-year-old lady who had survived the Nazi death camps. Kevin was warned by the family not to open the box 'under any circumstances', but he ignored the warning and opened the box. Kevin found a candlestick, two locks of human hair and a piece of paper with Yiddish writing inside.

Refusing to believe in the superstition surrounding the box, Kevin gave it to his mother as a present, but that is when things took a dark turn. His mother suffered a stroke, and when other sinister things occurred, such as rancid smells and shadowy features appearing, Kevin decided to sell it. The box was bought by a student, who also felt uneasy with the box in his possession, so it was sold again to a museum curator called James Haxton.

Haxton was originally sceptical, but in due course he began to suffer from unexplained bloodshot eyes, bruises and rashes, and nightmares. Eventually he grew so terrified by the box that he asked for help from experts and rabbis, and they instructed him to contain the box in any way possible. Some even suggested he build a wooden ark lined with 24-karat gold, put the box inside and bury it somewhere.

Today the box can be viewed behind a glass case at the Haunted Museum in Las Vegas, where it continues to have a strange effect on staff and visitors there. Zak Bagans, the *Ghost Adventures* TV star who owns and runs the museum, bought the box in 2017. In 2018, rap star Post Malone accidentally touched it in a private viewing. He reported a series of accidents and unfortunate events afterwards, including a car crash and an attempted armed robbery.

In 2021, Mannis admitted that the story behind the box was his own creation and that he had intended it over the years to become 'an interactive horror story evolving in real time'. Despite this admission, stories about the box and the evil presence trapped inside it linger on and on. Not to mention that anyone who wants to view it today must be an adult and sign a waiver beforehand!

69. CURSED RELICS

By its nature, every museum exhibit is haunted by the history and stories associated with it, but there are some ancient exhibits that are also strongly linked with paranormal energy. Many of these have become notorious, and one of the reasons they end up safely locked away in a museum is so they can't cause the harm they allegedly inflicted when in the real world.

The Hope diamond is perhaps the most famous diamond in the world. It originated in the Kollur Mine in Andhra Pradesia, India. According to legend, the stone is cursed because it was stolen from the eye of a sacred statue and will bring bad luck to anyone who owns it. The thief who stole the diamond met a gruesome death, and those who owned it afterwards experienced a series of catastrophes, including bankruptcy, murder and imprisonment. Eventually the diamond was donated to the Smithsonian Museum in 1958, with no apparent paranormal activity after its confinement.

A coffin was discovered in the 1800s in Thebes containing the mummy of a wealthy woman who lived around 900 BC. The mummy acquired a reputation for being unlucky and causing death and disaster for those who were in possession of it as well as those who were intrigued by it. In the early twentieth century, journalist William Thomas Stead wrote an article about the cursed mummy. He was one of the doomed passengers on the *Titanic* and allegedly told stories of the curse on the ship, causing some to believe he took the mummy's curse with him.

The Terracotta Army is an exquisite example of funeral art sculpture and was buried with the first Emperor of China, Qin Shi Huang, around 200 BC. It consists of an 8,000-strong army of soldiers, 130 chariots with 520 horses and 150 cavalry horses – and the bones of the thousands of workers who crafted the army before being buried alive with their emperor. It was discovered by farmers digging for water in 1974, and they feared that disturbing the army would bring misfortune. Indeed, their 2,000-year-old village was pulled down to make way for a museum, and each member of the group has, one by one, died penniless or been forced to earn a pittance working in the museum gift shop.

The Goddess of Death statue is an odd torso-shaped piece of limestone dating back to 3500 BC. It was discovered in Cyprus in 1878, and each of the families who owned it appeared to be cursed by unexpected death. Within six years of possessing it, all seven members of the first family had died, and the second owner died within four years. The same fatal misfortune befell families who bought it after that, until it was wisely donated to the Royal Scottish Museum.

The Great Bed of Ware at the Victoria and Albert Museum

in London was originally made for King Edward IV and is said to be cursed by the ghost of its architect, Jonas Fosbrooke, who felt disrespected by those who did not admire it, scratching and pinching guests until they were forced to find somewhere else to sleep. Busby's stoop chair, which can be found in the Thirsk Museum in Yorkshire, England, is also believed to be cursed by the ghost of Thomas Busby, who was hanged for a double murder in 1702. He cursed his favourite chair at a local inn, saying that anyone who sat on it would die. During the Second World War, airmen who sat in Busby's cursed chair were said never to return from their missions, and the chair was also linked to several accidents and illnesses. In 1978, the inn's landlord removed the chair to Thirsk Museum, where, ever since, the 'Dead Man's Chair' has been suspended high above the ground to make sure no poor unsuspecting soul ever sits in it again.

70. THE CURSED PAINTING

In 1972, Bill Stoneman's first wife, Rhoann, wrote a poem called 'Hands Resist Him'. It tells the haunting story of how Bill was adopted and did not know who his biological siblings were. The couple were living in California at the time, and Bill was an artist under contract with art gallery owner Charles Feingarten. Bill decided to use his wife's poem and an old photograph of himself as a child as inspiration for a painting.

When that photograph was taken, Stoneman was staying at his grandfather's apartment in Chicago. Conditions were cramped and squalid, and young Bill had to sleep on the floor in a closet. His father was often absent, as he travelled for his advertising job. Bill made friends and often played with a neighbour's young daughter. One day his parents took a photo of the two of them standing in front of a glass-paned door, against which there appear to be many hands or strange objects pressed. Stoneman painted the photograph and titled it *The Hands Resist Him*. The painting was put on display at an art gallery exhibition in 1974, where it was reviewed by art critic Henry Seldis and purchased by John Marley, famous for his role as producer for the movie *The Godfather*.

The painting disappeared from public view after Marley's death in 1984 but was tracked down two decades later, abandoned behind a former California brewery that had been reinvented as an art gallery. In 2000, a family who placed the painting on eBay included a horrific story in their online listing.

The family claimed that the painting was cursed and their children had seen the boy climb out of the painting at night. Not surprisingly, this led to a frenzy of interest in the painting online, with some viewers of the product complaining of hearing voices and feeling unwell afterwards. Eventually the painting was sold to Michigan gallery owner Kim Smith, but not before the legend of the terror it could inflict on anyone who even glanced at it online had gone viral.

Today, the terrifying painting remains at Smith's gallery, where it is kept in safe storage and only open to selective viewings. Haunted Museum owner Zak Bagans attempted but failed to purchase it for his collection of possessed objects, but Stoneman, who said he felt mystically connected to Bagans, painted a prequel for him. This prequel depicts the inside of the window from the original with the artist as a boy holding a paintbrush, called *The Hands that Invent Him*.

71. THE DEVIL'S ROCKING CHAIR

This is the true story of a rocking chair believed to belong to the devil. There is a debate about its origin, but it appears to have first surfaced in the early 1950s in Brookland, Connecticut, in the possession of the Glatzel family. For the next thirty or so years nothing remarkable happened concerning the chair, but that all changed in the summer of 1980.

In July 1980, David Glatzel, who was aged eleven at the time, was allegedly possessed by a demon. He would frequently wake up in the night screaming with terror and claiming that he had been visited by a man with a gaunt face, black eyes, pointed ears, sharp teeth, horns and hooves. The man told David that he was going to claim his soul.

Unexplained sounds coming from the attic were heard by witnesses when David was asleep, and bruises and cuts appeared on the terrified young boy. Things took an even more menacing step forward when the demon began to appear to David in broad daylight, often sitting in the family rocking chair. The family began to notice that the apparently empty chair would start rocking by itself. David also began to behave strangely, talking nonsense as well as quoting lines from the Bible and *Paradise Lost*. During the night he repeatedly woke up with seizures, so a family member had to be with him at all times.

The family asked a priest to bless the house, but things didn't improve. In desperation they turned to famous demonologists Ed and Lorraine Warren, who investigated the house and declared that forty-two demons and the devil were attacking the boy. They brought a priest with them to perform exorcisms, and all agreed that the rocking chair had a life of its own, moving of its own accord and even levitating in the air. Some of the exorcisms happened when David was sitting in the chair.

After one last exorcism extending over several days, the demon finally left David. But the terror continued, as it allegedly entered his sister Debbie's fiancé, Arne Johnson. Arne started to growl and hiss and suddenly go into deep trances. A few months later the formerly timid Arne savagely stabbed and killed his landlord, Alan Bono. He was arrested and charged with murder but entered a plea of not guilty based on demonic possession. Arne's plea made history, as it was the first time inhuman possession was taken seriously as a line of defence for a murder charge. However, the judge could find no evidence of possession and found him guilty. He was sent to prison but only served five years because of 'good behaviour', marrying Debbie on his release.

The rocking chair stayed with the Glatzel family. They took it with them whenever they moved. It was, however, largely kept in storage, because many who sat on it began to report excruciating back pain afterwards. It became the inspiration for *The Devil in Connecticut*, a book written about the case by the Warrens and

Gerald Brittle, as well as the film *The Conjuring: The Devil Made Me Do It*. Eventually it was sold, and today the stained, shabby-looking Devil's Rocking Chair, as it is now known, is lodged at the Haunted Museum in Las Vegas.

There is strong reason to believe that David suffered from mental illness and Arne from anger management and alcohol issues rather than demonic possession. In addition, the Glatzels sued the Warrens and Brittle for unspecified financial damages, claiming media attention and financial reward were the investigators' true motivators. Despite this, both staff and visitors at the Haunted Museum continue to report feelings of dread in the presence of the rocking chair. It has even caused fainting fits, so from time to time, for the wellbeing of both staff and visitors, the exhibit is temporarily removed from public display.

72. MORE ANGUISHED ART

The owner of the painting *The Anguished Man*, Sean Robinson, stated that he inherited the disturbing picture from his grandmother. Apparently his grandmother told him that the unknown artist of the painting had used his own blood mixed with paint to create the picture. That artist died by taking his own life soon after completing the painting.

In 2010, Sean uploaded a video of the picture online and claimed that he had heard unexplained sobbing noises in his home ever since owning the painting. He and several family members had also seen the shadowy figure of a man in his house. In 2015, in response to growing interest in the painting and the film rights being bought for the story, Sean declared that he had no intention of ever selling the painting, because he felt it was alive. People who have come into contact with the painting have described sudden nausea and nosebleeds, and Sean reported the experiences getting worse, with 'howling coming from the corner of our bedroom. We started to see the dark figure standing on the bottom of the bed, just staring at us.' Believing the painting to be 'dangerous', in the best interests of everyone, he has now stored it away in a secret location.

The backstory of the painting has been researched by parapsychologists, but, as is often the case with alleged haunted paintings, the evidence is largely anecdotal. Having said that, it is clear that for Sean and those who believe him, the story is real.

In some cases, logical explanations can be found for such anguished art. For example, prints of *The Crying Boy* by twentieth-century painter Giovanni Bragolin were believed to be cursed and the cause of a number of house fires in the 1980s. *The Crying Boy* prints were left undamaged by those fires, but this may simply be because the prints were treated with a fire-resistant varnish, and when they fell from the wall they landed face down, protecting them from the flames. However, this still doesn't explain why fires tended to break out in the homes where the prints were hanging.

A signed self-portrait by serial killer John Wayne Gacy, depicting his ghastly alter ego Pogo the Clown, was purchased by musician Nikki Stone for $3,000 in 2001. Soon afterwards, Stone's mother got cancer and his dog died, and he linked these misfortunes to the painting. A friend offered to put the painting in storage but later attempted to take their own life. Although it is possible the painting carried with it a dark energy that somehow attracted anguish into the lives of those who came into contact with it, perhaps it wasn't the painting in itself that was the magnet for negativity but the disturbing desire to own a self-portrait painted by a serial killer.

73. MANDY

Mandy the doll was created around 1910. The vintage porcelain doll with a cracked face, empty eyes, sinister half-smile and white frilly baby clothes was gifted to the Quesnel and District Museum in Canada in 1991 by a donor who chose to remain anonymous. The donor was eager to be rid of the doll after apparently hearing cries that sounded like a baby's coming from the basement where the doll had been stored.

The terrified owner heard the crying go on for several hours and finally found the courage to go down to the basement and investigate. When they entered the basement, the crying immediately stopped and they found nothing out of place there, except that the window was open. Although this was the only incident concerning the doll, it unsettled the owner so much that they eagerly handed Mandy over to the care of the museum.

As soon as the doll was put on display with other historical dolls, both staff and visitors to the museum began to report hearing footsteps and feeling inexplicably unsettled and distressed. Sometimes in the morning, staff would discover that dolls that had been standing on display around Mandy had toppled over in the night. Some suggested Mandy didn't like to share her space with them, so she was placed in her own special glass case.

In 1999, the strange antics surrounding Mandy were featured in a book entitled *Supernatural Stories around British Columbia*. This publicity ignited a great deal of interest in the doll, with museum visitors eager to see her and take photographs of her if they could. Many who tried to photograph her, however, said their cameras mysteriously switched off or malfunctioned or their batteries suddenly died. Others said Mandy's eyes seemed to follow them, and on one occasion the little toy lamb that sits on her lap somehow ended up outside the case. To this day those who visit Mandy in the museum continue to report feeling uneasy in her presence.

Thankfully, none of the alleged activity that clusters around Mandy appears to be deadly. The evidence for this activity is entirely anecdotal, but this doesn't stop visitors flocking to take a look at the doll for themselves. Psychics who have attempted to connect with the energy of the doll have suggested the spirit of a young girl who simply craves loving attention has attached itself to the doll. There is no proof, but this paranormal theory could explain why Mandy is mischievous but never violent. As long as she is the centre of attention, kept safe, allowed to play some harmless pranks and not ignored, laughed at or, most important of all, placed alone in a dark basement, she is content.

74. 200 DEMON HOUSE

In November 2011, Latoya Ammons, along with her mother, Rosa Campbell, and her three young children moved into a Carolina Street property in Gary, Indiana. The street was a quiet one, but a few days after moving in, the new arrivals discovered that their enclosed porch was swarming with massive black flies. They managed to kill the flies, but the insects kept returning. Not long afterwards, they heard the sound of heavy footsteps coming from the basement when nobody was down there. The basement door also kept opening by itself until they locked it firmly shut. Rosa reported waking one night to find a shadowy male figure pacing around her living room; on investigating further, she found large wet bootprints.

Things took a darkly dramatic turn when Latoya's twelve-year-old daughter allegedly began to levitate above Latoya's head while unconscious – it was only the collective prayer of family and friends that appeared to bring her back down. When she did return to earth, she said she had no memory of her flight.

Latoya reached out to local churches for help. One priest told her to draw crosses on all the windows and doors using oil. The family also burned sage around the house and read passages from the Bible at a makeshift altar. This led to a brief respite in activity, but the events soon intensified again. Mediums were approached, and one believed that over 200 demons had infected the house and that the best option was for the family to move and the house to be demolished. The family didn't have the funds to move.

As events progressed, Latoya became convinced her children were possessed by demons – she claimed that when possessed, their faces, voices and personalities changed completely. They would speak in harsh, deep voices and their faces would contort into evil shapes as they thrashed about uncontrollably. The children also claimed to speak to spirits. They would scream disturbing statements, such as 'I will kill you'. Over time, Latoya also succumbed to demonic possession herself and was prone to sudden fits of sweating and shaking. The grandmother claimed that the reason she was not possessed was that her guardian spirit was protecting her.

At times the family moved into a nearby hotel simply to find respite from the trauma. Medical staff present during the demonic trances witnessed the children levitating and being thrown against a wall. Other witnesses claimed to have actually seen one of the children climb the wall and backflip down from it, like Spider-Man.

Eventually, in 2012, the distressed family found a priest

dedicated to helping them exorcise their demons. He visited the house and confirmed it was infested with demons and also haunted by restless ghosts. He performed several exorcisms in both Latin and English, and for both the house and the family, to cast out the unclean spirits. The weird disturbances and personality changes stopped and never troubled the family again.

One physician who visited the house during the supposed demonic possession described the behaviour of the children as 'delusional'. He and the Department of Child Services were alarmed by the harrowing and inexplicable turn of events and believed the children were performing for their mother and for the attention and there could be mental health issues. This was perhaps the most unusual case ever investigated by the child services department, involving the fascinating collection of dozens of statements and documents from priests, police, doctors, psychologists, family members and eyewitnesses.

The house was demolished in 2016, but not before ghost hunter Zak Bagans had filmed a compelling documentary about the case, entitled *Demon House*. To this day, Latoya and many others remain convinced they actually encountered demons. Being a relatively recent case of alleged demonic activity, there is stacks of material online to pore over if you'd like to draw your own conclusions about 200 Demon House.

75. THE DEMON OF CLUMBER PARK

In the winter of 2022, a local couple were walking their dogs through an allegedly haunted forest in Clumber Park, Nottinghamshire, when they believe they captured footage of a 'demon ghost' crawling grotesquely in front of them on the path they were following.

According to newspaper reports, Hannah and Dave Rowett were up and out early one cold winter morning to take their dogs for a walk. As Dave was taking the Labradors out of the car, Hannah felt they were not alone. She instinctively reached for her phone and captured what appeared to be a shadowy figure crawling across the path in front of her. Later when she viewed the footage back with Dave, they immediately noticed that the figure resembled a long-limbed demon ghost.

Hannah believes there is no other logical explanation and is convinced she captured a demon on camera. Dave, a paranormal sceptic, is also at a loss to explain what Hannah filmed. Indeed, many who have viewed the image online struggle to explain it too, and while some declare it to be a trick of the light or a wild dog, others are convinced it is visual evidence that ghosts exist.

Clumber Park is rich in legends of ghosts and hauntings, and according to lore it is haunted by the ghost of a 'grey lady', who has been spotted emerging from the mist wearing a long grey cloak. The case of the Demon of Clumber Park is notable because of the important lesson it offers all budding paranormal investigators out there. Hannah didn't hesitate and switched her camera on when she sensed something uncanny. She admits she is a firm believer in an afterlife and from childhood has sensed the presence of ghosts, but this time when she sensed something invisible and out of this world she didn't just hope people would take her word for it, she decided to document it.

Cameras can sometimes capture things you can't see with the naked eye, and Hannah has what she believes to be proof – something tangible and credible that she can actually show people to help them believe. Although there is some debate about what can be seen in Hannah's picture, the general consensus online is that the image is something other than a wild dog or an animal, and it does not appear to have been edited. At the very least in this case, there is more than anecdotal evidence for paranormal enthusiasts.

76. ROLAND DOE

The chilling 1949 case of Roland or Robbie Doe – real name Ronald Hunkeler, as his identity was hidden at the time – was the inspiration for the 1971 novel *The Exorcist*, which two years later became the deeply disturbing and unforgettable movie of the same name.

Roland was an only child from a dysfunctional family who raised him in Cottage City, Maryland, in the US. He was close to his aunt, who introduced him to a Ouija board that he would often play with. On her death, Roland's family began to experience strange things happening in their home. It started with guttural noises and inexplicable knocking and then progressed to objects flying through the air. Roland's parents noticed that these things only happened in the presence of Roland, and they also claimed they saw him thrown into the air by his mattress.

The family asked their local pastor for help, and Roland was sent to stay at the pastor's home so he could observe him overnight. The pastor witnessed the flying household objects and advised the family to call in Catholic priests. Roland endured many exorcisms from this point onwards, as the priests believed his body needed to be rid of the demons possessing it.

There are eyewitness accounts which describe Roland's bed shaking, objects inexplicably levitating, and Roland swearing obscenities in an uncanny guttural voice and breaking free of his restraints to attack the exorcising priest. Roland also recoiled in terror whenever presented with a crucifix or readings from the Bible.

Unable to expel the evil spirits at his home, Roland was admitted to Georgetown University Hospital, a psychiatric hospital. Priests noticed that the words 'hell', 'spite' and 'evil' would spontaneously appear on his flesh, and he was prone to violent outbursts. One of the attending priests was allegedly so disturbed by what he witnessed that he was also admitted to the hospital, but there are no records of this admission. There are records, however, of Ronald's admission during the period when the exorcisms were said to have taken place. These records state that he underwent extensive psychological and medical testing.

In early March 1949, Roland was declared recovered and discharged from hospital. He was sent back to his parents, but the disturbances and skin branding returned. At this point it was decided that further exorcisms needed to be performed, and the archdiocese agreed. Roland was taken to the Alexian Brothers Hospital in St Louis. Details are confusing after that, but it is clear that several exorcisms were performed and attending priests described the terrors they witnessed as 'demonic' in origin.

Eventually the so-called demon was exorcised and there were no further signs of possession. In May 1949, Roland wrote to one of the priests saying he was happy and had a new dog. He continued to live in Maryland as a devout Catholic and eventually a married father of three.

This extraordinary case was said to be chronicled in a diary by the priests who performed the exorcisms and was meant to be a guide for future exorcisms. The only evidence we have for this is anecdotal, as the Catholic Church has never released details of the story.

For years afterwards people who were involved in the case or worked at the hospitals Roland was admitted to shared stories of what they saw. Nurses mentioned cleaning up pools of vomit and urine and hearing demonic laughter. They also spoke of the room Roland was in always being ice cold, no matter their efforts to warm it. Indeed, this room remained locked and unentered for nearly thirty years after the final exorcisms before the entire hospital was demolished.

Hunkeler grew up to become a NASA engineer who worked on the Apollo Space Missions in the 1960s and patented a technology that helped space shuttle panels endure intense heat. He died in 2020 and, according to one of his friends, lived his life on edge, anxious with worry that his NASA colleagues might discover he was the inspiration for *The Exorcist*.

Sceptics can and do present a convincing case here for the explanation being mental illness, hallucination or trickery on the part of Roland, but whether you believe in demons or not, the only way to entirely dismiss this story is to say that everyone involved was either deluded or a liar. This seems unlikely given the number of priests and respected medical staff connected to the case who were absolutely convinced this was the work of the devil. The case remains an enigma, its details horrifying.

77. ANNELIESE MICHEL

The shocking events depicted in the 2005 film *The Exorcism of Emily Rose*, the 2006 movie *Requiem* and 2011's *Anneliese: The Exorcism Tapes* were all loosely based on the true story of a vulnerable German girl called Anneliese Michel.

Anneliese was raised in a devout Catholic household in Bavaria, south-east Germany, in the 1960s. One day, at the age of sixteen, she entered a trance-like state while at school. When she woke up from the trance, having walked around in a daze, she had no recollection of it. There were no further incidents until a year later when she entered a trance while in her bed, but this time she went into convulsions and wet herself.

After this disturbing development, Anneliese visited a neurologist who diagnosed her with temporal lobe epilepsy, a medical disorder that causes hallucinations, seizures and memory loss. She was put on medication and it appeared to help. But despite this, she soon started to believe the devil was trying to possess her and that the solution to her distressing situation lay outside medication. She claimed to hear demons whispering in her ears and to see the face of the devil.

Anneliese asked priests for help, but they urged her to visit her doctor and told her that an exorcism was not possible without the permission of the bishop. From then onwards Anneliese's behaviour became dangerously extreme. When she was 'possessed' she would rip her clothes off her body and crawl under the table licking the floor, eating insects and howling like a dog. She is even said to have eaten spiders and coal and bitten the head off a dead bird.

Eventually Anneliese and her mother found a priest called Ernst Alt who did not think she was an epileptic. He petitioned the local bishop and permission was granted for a secret exorcism by a local priest called Arnold Renz. For ten months after receiving the bishop's approval, Alt and Renz conducted a mind-boggling sixty-seven exorcisms on the vulnerable young woman, each one lasting hours. During these exorcisms, Anneliese screamed that she was possessed by six demons battling with each other to possess her: Lucifer, Cain, Nero, Judas, Hitler and a disgraced priest called Fleischmann. Anneliese would talk about 'dying to atone' for sinners in the world.

Over these ten gruelling months, Anneliese was restrained by the priests so they could perform their exorcisms. She broke bones in her knees through constant kneeling to pray and gradually stopped eating and drinking altogether. She died of starvation and dehydration on 1 July 1976 at only twenty-three years old.

Following her death, Anneliese's story became notorious in Germany and the exorcising priests were arrested and charged with homicide. In their trial, their defence was paid for by the Church, and the priests played recordings from the exorcisms in an attempt to justify their actions. They were found guilty of manslaughter by negligence and sentenced to six months in jail, which they never served, and three years of probation. Her parents – Joseph and Anna – were not punished either, as the judge believed they had already endured enough suffering.

Photographs from the sensational trial can be found online, as can images of the horrifying exorcisms performed on Anneliese. Anneliese had been diagnosed with mental illness and tragically paid the ultimate price for her guardians' misguided and ignorant intervention. For the great majority of people, they remain a tragic and disturbing warning of what happens when people project their superstitions and beliefs onto an extremely vulnerable person.

Despite this, as well as being a source for horror movies, Anneliese's story became an 'inspiration' for devout Catholics, who truly believed supernatural forces had been at work and that the exorcising priests had acted with integrity. Anneliese's grave became a pilgrimage site, with visitors leaving notes and lighting candles to thank her for bravely enduring the sins of the world. In their eyes, this was a case of demonic possession – an evil force possessing an innocent victim who died in her courageous refusal to allow them to do so.

78. THE BLACK MAUSOLEUM

Greyfriars Kirkyard Cemetery in Edinburgh is regarded by some paranormal experts to be the most haunted cemetery in Scotland, if not the world. Author Neil Gaiman found inspiration there for his *The Graveyard Book*, as did J. K. Rowling for Godric's Hollow, where Harry Potter's parents are buried. Rowling also used familiar names from gravestones there, such as Moodie and Thomas Riddell. However, it is the Black Mausoleum, also known as the Mackenzie tomb, that is perhaps most infamous in the cemetery.

In recent decades the Black Mausoleum, a small tomb located behind locked gates and high walls in an area formerly known as the Covenanter's Prison at Greyfriars Cemetery, has been associated with an evil demonic entity also known as the

Mackenzie poltergeist. However, this story sits more comfortably in the category of inhuman hauntings because of the number of documented sightings and the severity of them, from unrelated parties, suggesting there is no one human agent that the phenomena cluster around, as tends to be the case in typical poltergeist activity. Instead, it is the tomb that appears to be the locus of the hauntings.

Visitors to the tomb have reported cold chills, unexplained cuts and bruises, and burns – some happening under their clothes. There have also been sightings of the apparition of a white figure, mysterious knocking sounds and foul smells coming from within the tomb. Others have felt their hair being pulled by invisible forces. Unmarked bodies of dead animals have also been found near the Black Mausoleum. And this paranormal activity isn't just confined to the tomb itself – four different houses located close by have experienced unexplained fires.

The chilling associations with this tomb aren't as dated as you may think. Indeed, the first story surfaced in 1999, when a homeless man seeking shelter there claimed an unseen force had attacked him. From then on there have been around 200-and-counting documented reports, as well as features, books and televised ghost hunts. The *Harry Potter* association has also propelled the graveyard into the spotlight, making it a tourist destination.

Theories have been put forward to explain the sheer number of alleged paranormal incidents, and these include pheromones, mass hysteria, electromagnetic radiation from nearby machinery, geology and the overactive imaginations of *Harry Potter* fans. Psychics have suggested that the activity may be connected to the restless ghost of a seventeenth-century Lord Advocate Prosecutor of the Covenanters, known as George 'Bloody' Mackenzie, who is buried there. Mackenzie had a reputation for being utterly ruthless, often torturing and executing his enemies with cruel enthusiasm in the location of the tomb. A couple of hundred years later, John Hayes, a criminal on the run, allegedly hid in the Black Mausoleum for six months. When he was finally caught by the police, he had gone insane and spoke of hearing Mackenzie moving and scraping inside his coffin at night.

Occult experts believe the evil associations with the tomb are a magnet for demonic forces. A few people who have visited the tomb have claimed they felt possessed afterwards, and exorcisms have been performed at the tomb. In 2000, a medium attempted to lay to rest the evil ghost there, but he died of a heart attack a few weeks later. Some believe this to be the dark work of the Mackenzie poltergeist, but sceptics argue that surely the deadly power of fear and suggestion – rather than a vindictive evil entity – is at work here.

79. JULIA

A 2020 book, written by man of science Dr Richard Gallagher and entitled *Demonic Foes*, shows that belief in demonic possession is very much alive today. A Yale-trained and board-certified psychiatrist from New York, Dr Gallagher is currently regarded as the world's leading expert on the subject of diabolic attacks.

In his book, Gallagher details some truly shocking cases of modern-day possession and vividly describes the exorcisms he has witnessed during thirty years as an exorcist's consultant. The controversial conclusion Gallagher draws is that in extremely rare instances of reported demonic possession, something that is not psychosis or mental illness and which is outside his expertise as a board-certified psychiatrist is occurring.

Perhaps Gallagher's most extreme case involved a patient known by the pseudonym 'Julia'. He observed Julia – a satanist high priestess – for several months and during this time witnessed her speak in tongues, put a curse on his pet cats and levitate. Julia originally came to Gallagher's attention when she was brought to his door by a priest he knew. She had jet-black hair and eyeliner that stretched to her ears, and she asked him how his cats were. This shocked Gallagher because the night before, his normally docile cats had been fighting with each other and he had had to separate them.

Gallagher believes Julia exhibited behaviours that constituted possession, knowing personal details about his private life and speaking to him in her demonic voice even when she was miles away. In a consultation with him, Julia agreed, stating, 'I know I am possessed. I space out and then don't recall what happens. They tell me a voice comes out of me. I don't know. I don't remember anything. It's a demon. I'm sure.'

Julia's incredible case was among the first of many that Gallagher would diagnose in a long career devoted to distinguishing psychosis from alleged possession. Another case is 'Barbara', a tiny woman who was somehow able to throw a grown man across the room and who spoke Latin without any former knowledge of it. There was also 'Stan', whom he witnessed being choked by invisible hands.

Predictably, film rights to Julia's story have been sold. Gallagher believes that genuine cases of possession are extremely rare, but he is utterly convinced they can and do occur. He stresses that he is not trying to convince or alarm people by drawing this conclusion and that his motive in writing his book is simply to present the evidence he has gathered.

80. THE SMURL FAMILY HAUNTING

The Smurl family's story is a case of alleged demonic possession which appears to have sinisterly infected not just one human host but an entire family. Widely considered a hoax today, at the time it attracted widespread attention and was taken very seriously indeed by the demonologists investigating it and the priests who exorcised it.

In 1973, Jack's parents, John and Mary Smurl, bought a house on Chase Street in West Pittson, Pennsylvania, in the US. The house was a duplex built in 1896. John and Mary lived in one half, while their son, his wife Janet, and their two daughters Dawn and Heather moved into the second half.

For the first eighteen months they were one big happy family, but strange things began to occur in January 1974 when a mysterious stain appeared on the carpet. Water began to leak from pipes and unexplained scratches appeared on furniture. A TV set exploded and drawers opened, toilets flushed and radios played by themselves. The family also heard mysterious footsteps and noticed strange odours in the house. However, it wasn't until 1985 that things turned from annoying to disturbing.

In February 1985, the house turned icy cold and a loud and abusive disembodied voice was heard. Light fixtures fell from the ceiling. Jack started to levitate. Loud scratching sounds and footsteps were heard in the attic. Bedspreads were shredded.

In 1986, Janet was at her wits' end and contacted well-known demonologists Ed and Lorraine Warren. The Warrens investigated and concluded that the house was haunted by a demon and three minor spirits. Janet and her mother-in-law Mary allegedly saw a 5 feet 9 inches black human form looming over them in the kitchen. The Warrens believed this was a demon that had been dormant in the house for a century but had risen again to draw on the emotional energy generated by the Smurl daughters, Dawn and Heather, entering puberty.

The hauntings increased in severity. Jack and Janet reported that they had been 'raped' at night by demonic entities known as a succubus and an incubus. To make matters worse, the demon appeared to follow the Smurls when they left the house, removing the option of moving house to escape it.

Apparently desperate for help and frustrated by the refusal of the Catholic Church to intervene, the Smurls appeared on local Pennsylvania TV, anonymously interviewed behind a screen. The demon was not best pleased and the activity increased. By August 1986, with no respite from their trauma, the Smurls went public about their ordeal and gave an exclusive interview to the *Sunday Independent* newspaper. Curious visitors immediately flocked to their home.

Paul Kurtz, chairman of the Committee for the Scientific

Investigation of Claims into the Paranormal in Buffalo, New York, offered to put the family up in a hotel so he could observe what was going on with cameras. The Smurls refused, saying they believed there was no point because Kurtz had already made up his mind this was a hoax. Kurtz later wrote an article stating that the case was not paranormal and the Smurls had refused his investigation because they knew he would uncover the truth of their fraud. He said there was no record of Janet contacting the police when she said she had and that natural explanations, such as a broken sewer pipe creating the foul odour, an abandoned mine making echoing sounds, and teenage pranks, were the most likely explanations. He also suggested the possibility of hallucinations and urged the family to submit themselves for psychiatric evaluation. Kurtz also questioned whether there was a financial motive, as in 1986 the Smurls co-authored with the Warrens a book detailing their story and they were also in talks with TV producers.

The Warrens added to the scepticism surrounding this case by repeatedly declining reporters' requests to stay in the house to see for themselves or to allow anyone outside the family to watch alleged recordings of the phenomena. However, the intensive press coverage of the case eventually pushed the diocese into action, and the Warrens were granted permission to orchestrate a mass exorcism with several priests. The dramatic exorcism appears to have been entirely successful, because after thirteen years of the Smurl family apparently being at the mercy of repeated sinister disturbances, the activity ceased. In 1991, *Haunted*, a two-hour movie about the Smurl Haunting, was released, and since then the Smurl hauntings have continued to inspire other demonic dramas.

81. HIGHGATE CEMETERY

Opened in 1839, Highgate Cemetery occupies 20 acres on the south slope of Highgate village in London, England. It was built during an era when London churches could not cope with the huge numbers of burials required. During Victorian times it became a very fashionable place to be buried. The cemetery grounds are rich in wild flowers, animals, trees and above-ground Gothic tombs built in extravagant style. Thousands of people have been laid to rest there, including some famous names such as Karl Marx.

Rumours about satanic cults and meetings held in the cemetery ruins began after the Second World War, when local newspapers started to receive reports from terrified witnesses of paranormal encounters there. One man stated that when his car broke down outside the cemetery, he saw the apparition of a red-eyed demon staring at him through the cemetery fence. Another saw a loathsome creature glide through the walls of the cemetery and dissolve into thin air once outside. Others said they witnessed evil-looking mists emerging from graves and spectral faces floating on the pathway.

The ghost of a nun and a phantom cyclist have been reported several times, as has an elderly woman, but the most reported apparition appears to be the so-called Highgate vampire. In 1969, reports first surfaced of a 7 feet tall black apparition stalking the tombs, and over time others reported a similar looming and menacing hypnotic presence with blood-chilling red eyes standing behind them and lurking in the shadows.

Then the foxes in the area started dying, and a 1970 local press feature asked why. As some of the foxes were found with their throats cut, it was swiftly suggested that a vampire, who was formerly a medieval nobleman and practised black magic in Romania, was on the prowl in the cemetery. The story goes that this nobleman was buried at Highgate and was at peace there until a satanic ritual at the site awakened him. Not surprisingly, this led to a media circus, with paranormal detectives, journalists and TV crews bombarding the cemetery in the hope of capturing footage. Although anecdotal reports of terrifying screams and shadowy tall figures continued to be reported during this frenzy, no clear footage or proof was ever gathered.

Mass hysteria was the explanation put forward at the time, but things flared up again in August 1970. Two teenage girls said they had discovered the corpse of an elderly woman in the middle of the cemetery pathway; she had been removed from her coffin, decapitated and staked through the heart. Police suspected the body had been used for black magic. Reports of a tall figure in a black cloak resurfaced, with a number of witnesses telling stories of the figure pushing visitors to the cemetery to the ground.

An attempt to hold a seance and an exorcism to banish the evil entities haunting Highgate was thrown into disarray when the police arrived on the scene in protest. Sightings of the Highgate vampire in particular dwindled dramatically after that aborted seance. However, over the years, visitors to the cemetery continue to report feelings of dread and sudden drops in temperature. There are also reports of watches and mobiles malfunctioning within the cemetery walls.

82. THE CECIL HOTEL

Given the number of suicides, murders and accidental deaths that have occurred at the infamous Cecil Hotel, many ghost hunters believe it to be a magnet for paranormal activity. At the very least, the hotel's disturbing past lends itself exceedingly well to reports of evil energies lurking there.

Located in downtown Los Angeles in the US, close to Skid Row (a neighbourhood known for its condensed population of homeless people), the Cecil Hotel was built in the 1920s. The hotel fell into decline following the Great Depression in America in the 1930s and earned a seedy reputation as a refuge for drug addicts, sex workers and the down and out.

Over the years, multiple tragedies and crimes have been linked to the hotel. These include the 1947 unsolved murder of aspiring actress Elizabeth Short, also known as the Black Dahlia, who was last seen at the Cecil Hotel before her mutilated body was discovered in a nearby park. Many suicides by jumping from the hotel windows have been reported. One of those suicides, in 1962, also caused the death of an innocent passer-by, struck by someone who had jumped from the window above. A young mother murdered her newborn baby there by throwing the baby out of the window, and in 1964, a local eccentric woman known for feeding pigeons was found brutally murdered and sexually assaulted there.

Perhaps the most well-known evil presence to rent a $14-a-night top-floor room in the hotel on a regular basis was serial killer Richard Ramirez, who sexually assaulted and murdered numerous people between 1984 and 1985. He became known as the Night Stalker because his crimes, committed in the dead of the night, terrorized Los Angeles residents. After killing his victims, he allegedly returned to the hotel with bloodstained clothes, which he threw into a dumpster behind the hotel before returning to his room stark naked. Due to the rundown, crime-infested nature of the hotel, his bizarre behaviour went unnoticed.

Ramirez wasn't the only serial killer drawn to the Cecil Hotel. In 1991, Jack Unterweger, an Austrian man suspected of killing scores of sex workers in Austria and the United States, stayed at the Cecil Hotel to write a feature about sex workers for an Austrian magazine. It is said he sought out the Cecil Hotel as a sordid tribute to Ramirez, and after his stay he went on to kill three American sex workers.

And then there was the grisly discovery of the body of Canadian student Elisa Lam in one of the hotel's water tanks. The twenty-one-year-old Columbian woman stayed at the hotel and was reported missing on 31 January 2013. In early February her disappearance was investigated by police, who found she suffered from depression and bipolar disorder. They released a now famous video of her looking as if she was hiding from someone in one of the hotel lifts, appearing to interact with someone out of view, and pressing multiple elevator buttons before stepping into and out of the lift with erratic movements. Her body was discovered on 19 February in one of the water tanks on the roof of the hotel after, in a particularly grisly detail, guests complained of low water pressure and toxic-tasting water.

Lam's case sparked endless theories about how on earth she ended up in the water tank, as it is a steep and dangerous climb to the top and would require tremendous strength to lift the tank's lid. Some paranormal experts believe that Ramirez, who was allegedly a satanist, may have caused a demonic presence to infect the hotel, which then took possession of Lam. Although the case was declared an accidental drowning, speculation as to what or who caused her death has continued, inspiring the 2021 Netflix series *Crime Scene: The Vanishing at the Cecil Hotel*.

83. RUFFORD ABBEY

Rufford Abbey, in Nottinghamshire, England, was originally a sixteenth-century Cistercian abbey, though it was converted to a country estate after King Henry VIII's dissolution of the monasteries. It stands out for the frequency of ghostly sightings, with multiple unexplained images of spirits captured at the abbey.

A white lady ghost reportedly spotted there is believed to be the residual ghost of Lady Arbella Stuart, a noble woman considered to be in line for the throne, especially when she married another claimant to the throne, William Seymour. Arbella visited the abbey around 1609 before she was taken to her death in the Tower of London. The most terrifying haunting, however, is that of an evil entity known as the Satanic Monk, a tall, sinister figure in a black monk's cowl.

According to lore, during the medieval period the abbey was

originally home to an order of Cistercian monks who wore white. One of the monks came into contact with a grimoire (book) of satanic spells which detailed how to raise, summon and command demons and even the devil himself. The monk became obsessed with the book and tried to translate it into Latin. He was caught in the act of translation and horrifically punished by his own order. His entire head was scalped, leaving his eyes in their sockets so a mirror could be held up for him to see his ghastly reflection. Incredibly, the monk did not faint or die from the scalping. He was then chained and buried alive under a stone slab in the cellar, where he died an agonizingly slow death. The grimoire was wrapped in the skin that had been peeled from his skull and then burned.

The monk's evil apparition is said to haunt Rufford Abbey, with eyewitness reports mentioning a figure with a bloodied bare skull, red eyes and a black tongue that curses all who encounter him. A gravestone in nearby Edwinstowe churchyard is the final resting place of Francis Thompson, who is said to have died of fright after seeing the monk in 1898.

Whether or not the story of the Satanic Monk is true – and whether or not this entry falls into the residual or demonic inhuman category – is debatable, but one thing appears certain: many visitors have reported feelings of dread at Rufford Abbey. Here is what Andrew Pollard, AKA Yorkshire Ghost Guy, who has been actively investigating the possibility of an afterlife since the death of his father in 2003, recently recounted:

Nothing could have prepared me for just how active and unnerving Rufford Abbey would turn out to be … It started when I participated in a table tipping session in the Cellarium. The experience was so disturbing that I have not been able to take part in this kind of spirit communication again. During the session a black mist was trying to manifest, much like a black whirlwind or tornado. I also felt myself grabbed by unseen hands. Even stranger things happened. A very heavy table in the Frater where the monks used to eat creaked as it levitated. A wooden hammer from a xylophone flew through the air, hitting me on the leg. In addition to witnessing unexplained foul smells, and the words 'Get Out' written by unseen hands in a tray of white chalk dusk, we also heard a frightening growl coming from the Cellarium when it was empty. Since then I have not returned to Rufford due to how uneasy the place makes me feel.

84. A DEMON MADE ME DO IT

In 1974, Yorkshireman Michael Taylor sensationally claimed he was possessed by demons – and that those demons made him kill his wife.

Taylor's wife, Christine, had told their Christian Fellowship Group that she was having problems with her husband, who she alleged was cheating on her with the leader of the group, Marie Robinson. Together Michael and twenty-one-year-old Marie would engage in private rituals, making the sign of the cross at each other to, as they said, ward off the evil power of the full moon. Christine reported that her once easy-going husband had become increasingly surly and argumentative. Michael was summoned and questioned by his local vicar and other ministers. When he started to behave erratically and speak in tongues, attacking Marie, it was decided that an exorcism needed to be performed to cast out the evil within him. Marie reported that when Michael assaulted her, 'he looked almost bestial. He kept looking at me and there was a really wild look in his eyes.'

Between 5 and 6 October 1974, Father Peter Vincent, an

Anglican priest assisted by Rev. Raymond Smith, a Methodist, performed an exorcism at St Thomas's Church. The priests believed that they invoked and cast out at least forty demons, including those of bestiality, incest and lewdness. After an exhausting two days, they let Michael return home but were concerned that at least three demons – violence, murder and insanity – were still lingering there within him. Tragically, they were proved correct.

Shortly afterwards, Michael murdered Christine. He killed her in cold blood, calmly ripping out her eyes and tongue with his bare hands. He was found by a policeman, wandering naked in the street and covered from head to toe in his wife's blood. As he was arrested, he was heard screaming over and over: 'It is the blood of Satan!' At his trial Taylor was acquitted on the grounds of insanity, with his lawyer arguing the fellowship group was little more than a cult feeding off Michael's pre-existing mental health issues. He was sent to a secure ward in Broadmoor Hospital and released a few years later.

The Taylor case attracted a huge amount of publicity at the time, as well as fears surrounding the insanity plea and claims of demonic possession being used to defend the indefensible. Perhaps this is best summed up in the words of the policeman who discovered the raving Taylor: 'Before this event I was agnostic … now I'm an atheist.'

85. HOUSES OF HORROR

It is not just people that can be allegedly possessed by evil entities – objects, animals, locations and buildings can be haunted too. Although there may have been a human agent (and potentially an animal one) in the case of the so-called Bridgeport Poltergeist, the house itself became yet another strong contender for the dubious accolade of the world's most haunted house.

In November 1974, an ordinary bungalow-style home on Lindley Street in Bridgeport, Connecticut, became the focus of one of the most witnessed hauntings in American history. The home was owned by Gerald (Jerry) and Laura Goodin, who stated that seriously weird things were happening behind their closed doors – objects levitating, windows shattering, an exploding crucifix and, most bizarrely of all, their pet cat was talking to them.

The intensity of the paranormal activity became so great that the police, firefighters, priests, members of the American Society for Psychical Research, and journalists repeatedly visited and investigated the house. Famous paranormal investigators Ed and Lorraine Warren were also called in. They claimed to hear disembodied voices and the voice of Sam, the family cat, saying 'jingle bells' and 'bye-bye'. Marcia, the couple's ten-year-old adopted daughter, was often at the centre of much of the activity, with an increase in the intensity of paranormal activity whenever she was in the house.

The Goodins claimed they did not believe in the paranormal and were at their wits' ends. They repeatedly called in the police to search for a cause, but nothing was ever discovered. Over time, as local and national press covered the haunting, thousands gathered around the house to try to catch a glimpse of the supernatural. Some tried to take matters into their own hands and perform exorcisms themselves.

Things eventually came to a head when one of the witnesses noticed Marcia kicking a TV over when she thought no one was watching. She immediately confessed to being the cause of the strange goings-on in the house, and the general consensus was that the entire thing had been a hoax. However, some continued to question how paranormal events they had witnessed with their own eyes had happened when Marcia was not in the house or had occurred in a room she was not in at the time. In addition, strange things continued to happen in the house for a few months after Marcia's confession.

Today, the current residents of the Lindley Street house have no interest in discussing its allegedly haunted history. The same desire for privacy can be said for a more recent haunting that took place in a house in Haverfordwest, Wales, purchased by a young couple as their 'dream' home in 1989. In 2015, paranormal author Gavin Lee Davies wrote the bestselling book *A Most Haunted House*, which recounts in vivid and harrowing detail how living in a home believed to be haunted by an unknown evil presence tore his relationship and life apart. The book explores numerous possible explanations, including that it could all have happened in the author's mind, but the lasting impression left on the reader is that the experience was real and that something out of this world possessed Gavin's 'dream' home.

86. THE SEA OF TREES

The 'sea of trees' is the name given to Aokigahara, a spooky and atmospheric Japanese forest dense with trees. It is located north-west of Mount Fuji and stretches over 13 miles. Sadly, it has also earned itself another nickname: 'Suicide Forest'.

Every year an estimated 100 people enter the forest and take their lives. Indeed, the risk of visitors taking their own lives is deemed to be so high that volunteers patrol the edges of the forest to offer help if needed and also to warn them of the dangers of entering the forest.

The forest is strangely quiet, and because it is so dense, it can barely sustain any wildlife. The stillness feels suffocating to those who are brave enough to enter and the silence unnerving. There are many eerie cave openings in the forest, and the floor is hard, rocky and impenetrable. Phones routinely malfunction – some have suggested that it is the iron-rich soil messing with the signals. Others believe the forest is home to evil demonic forces, and visitors bold enough to enter are advised to mark their way clearly so they can safely find their way out again. There have been reports, though, of the markers being sabotaged and tape being cut by unseen hands.

According to lore, it is the spirits of those who took their own lives there that remain trapped in this unforgiving forest. There is also the belief that inhuman demons feed on the negative feelings of those who enter and lure them deep into the forest, where they lose their minds. Paranormal investigators have reported seeing white floating figures slithering between the twisted branches of the trees, and some of these images have been captured on camera. There have also been a number of mysterious finds in the forest, including abandoned backpacks, ripped clothing and, most chilling of all, human bones.

The forest's nickname 'sea of trees' sounds innocent, but it carries with it a menacing association. According to Japanese lore, areas and places associated with water, such as rivers and seas, are plagued by the so-called Kappa demon, an unpredictable turtle-like entity with a cavity on its head that must always be filled with water, because if it is spilled, the Kappa will die. The Kappa is said to be friendly at times, but more often than not it is menacing, known to attack and drown people and animals, especially when the areas of water are not respected and kept clean.

Whether associated with supernatural forces or not, the tragedy of Aokigahara cannot be denied and is made clear to all who enter by prominent signs which read: 'Your life is a precious gift from your parents. Please think about your parents, siblings and children. Don't keep it to yourself. Talk about your troubles.'

87. GHOST TOWNS

There is always something eerie about towns and cities that have been abandoned. Frozen in time, they evoke an atmosphere of mystery and desolation that lends itself incredibly well to stories of hauntings.

This is most certainly the case for Al Jazirat Al Hamra in the United Arab Emirates. It was once a bustling and beautiful fishing village, but it was totally abandoned in the 1960s. Some say this is because demons and ghosts drove the villagers out. To this day, legend dictates that evil *djinns* wander the ruins disguised as animals, and visitors have also reported witnessing apparitions and hearing strange wailing sounds as the sun goes down on the derelict remains of this once thriving town.

Another apparently haunted ghost town is La Noria in northern Chile, located in the Atacama Desert. It was built in 1826 and was once a busy mining town with thousands of residents and its own railway station, school and other amenities. Conditions for the mining families were incredibly tough, and many died working in the scorching heat. The town started to fall into decline in the early 1900s, and by the time the First World War broke out, its saltpetre resources had depleted dramatically. The resident mining families had no alternative but to leave.

Many La Noria residents appear to have left in a hurry, leaving their possessions behind and making the ghost town ripe for looting and vandalism. Even coffins have been dug up to steal any jewellery or other valuables that may have been buried with the corpses. Visitors today can still see the gruesome sight of exposed bodies and scattered bones in the graveyard. With the peace of the dead shattered in this way, it is no surprise that the place is considered a paranormal hotspot and a magnet for evil energy. There have been reports of the dead rising from their graves at sunset to investigate the ruins of their former home. Visitors to the town in daylight have also reported feeling inexplicable panic and dread and hearing disembodied footsteps and blood-curdling screams.

Another former mining town created in the 1850s but abandoned by the mid-twentieth century is Golden in southern Oregon, near Wolf Creek in the US. A visit there is a fascinating adventure into what life was like in that part of America over 150 years ago, with the remaining buildings still containing tools and other objects from villagers' day-to-day lives, abandoned as if it were yesterday. No surprise, it is a favourite location for ghost hunters, with visitors reporting hearing eerie voices and witnessing shadowy figures lurking in the dark.

La Noria, Golden and Al Jazirat Al Hamra are just three of countless haunted ghost towns I could have included here. You will be surprised just how many abandoned towns and cities there are all over the world. And all of them are utterly unique, with their own distinctive ghosts and spirits.

88. THE BERMUDA TRIANGLE

In 1945, six American Air Force planes and their entire crews mysteriously vanished on a calm day with ideal flying conditions in an infamous area of the ocean just east of Florida known as the Bermuda Triangle.

The mysterious history of the Bermuda Triangle dates back to Italian explorer Christopher Columbus, known for his 1492 'discovery' of the new land of the Americas on board his ship, *Santa Maria*. While sailing through the area, Columbus and his crew were unnerved by bolts of lightning, eerie lights and the compass going wild. Over the years, the area has become notorious for strange occurrences. Until 1945, it was thought only ships were affected, but since then mysterious happenings have affected not just ships but planes, and up to 1,000 people have simply vanished when entering this restricted section of the ocean.

Accidents and mishaps happen at sea, but they apparently occur more often here than anywhere else and also apparently when weather conditions are ideal. Most mysterious of all, no trace of wreckages, survivors or bodies are recovered. Common to many of the disappearances is that no distress calls are sent from the crew. Like the *Mary Celeste*, some ships have even been found days later, undamaged and seaworthy but eerily floating entirely deserted by the crew – to be known forevermore as ghost ships. The disappeared crew members are never heard from again.

On 22 December 1967, the cabin cruiser *Witchcraft* left Miami with her captain Dan Burack and his friend Father Patrick Horgan. The two men were intent on enjoying the view of Miami's Christmas lights. But after reaching 1 mile offshore, they called the coast guard saying their ship had hit something, although they didn't think it was seriously damaged. The coast guard set off immediately, intending to tow the ship to safety, and reached the location of *Witchcraft* in under twenty minutes. On arrival, the cruiser was nowhere to be found.

Witchcraft was a well-equipped vessel with many life-saving devices on board, including lifeboats, life jackets, distress signals and so forth. In coming days, the coast guard searched hundreds of square miles of the ocean but found nothing. To this day, no trace of those on board the doomed cruiser has ever been found.

The US government keeps a watchful eye on the Bermuda Triangle, but despite being policed, the number of disappearances far exceeds chance for such a small area of the ocean. All the most obvious causes have been explored – weather, human error and so on – but all have fallen short of offering a definitive explanation. This has led some paranormal experts to suggest that the 'vanishments' could be caused by time slips, vengeful ghosts or inhuman demons, spirits, elementals or other unexplained entities or forces.

89. TIME SLIPS

In August 1911, two British women visited the Palace of Versailles in France and claimed to have been thrown right back in time to the eighteenth century.

The two women were on an organized tour of the palace but decided to do their own sightseeing. They walked down an alleyway and found themselves feeling very heavy physically, and then for a few moments they stepped into another time. It looked unnatural. The people they met were like waxworks, the scenery without life and light, and they met a blonde woman wearing old-fashioned clothing. It took a while for them to process what had happened to them that day. Each time they retraced their steps, they could not find the alleyway they had walked down.

Ten years later, they published a book about it called *An Adventure*. The book was a bestseller but wasn't taken seriously. Undaunted by naysayers, the friends remained convinced that they had stepped back in time to a few weeks before the French Revolution and that the blonde woman they had met was none other than Marie Antoinette.

The issue with time travel stories is not just that the evidence is always anecdotal but that they are an open invitation for fiction and fact to merge. The story of the so-called Times Square time traveller back in 1950 is a case in point. A man was hit and killed by a car in Times Square, but when his body was taken to the morgue, he was wearing and carrying items that belonged to a previous century and carried a letter with an 1876 postmark and the name Rudolph Fentz, which was later proved legitimate. Sounds thrilling, were it not for the fact that it never happened and was actually the plot of a short story by Jack Finney called *I'm Scared*, which somehow merged into urban legend.

There is one story, though, that is less easily written off and that involves a bearded Caucasian French-speaking man who travelled to Haneda Airport in July 1954 and handed over a passport issued in a country called Taured, which does not exist in real life. When challenged, the man was incredulous, saying this was his hometown and it had been in existence for a century. He pointed to Andorra on the map as the location of Taured. The man was arrested for suspicious behaviour and placed in a hotel room with two guards stationed outside. The next day, when the guards entered the room, the man had vanished. Could this have been a man from a parallel universe or the future who entered and exited through a portal, or is this again the work of a great storyteller?

Much more research needs to be done into time slip stories like those mentioned above, as well as doppelgänger stories, which involve meeting an older or a younger version of yourself or seeing an apparition of someone you know is alive in another location. Other symptoms of potential time slips include seeing shadowy figures, weird creatures and shapes in the corner of your eye and, last but by no means least, glowing orbs of light.

90. ORBS

Images of unexplained white or spherical glowing balls of light, or orbs, have often been associated with ghosts and hauntings, especially in recent years. A simple online search will reveal thousands of orb photographs, so you can take a look for yourself. For example, in 2020, an orb was caught on camera by a police chaplain in his Daytona Beach, Florida, home, leaving him with a whole new world of questions. In 2022, ghost hunters at the Ancient Ram Inn (see page 59) in England captured and published images and videos of unexplained orbs.

Although orbs have been reported for centuries and peaked in popularity during the era of Victorian spiritualism, the craze for capturing orbs on film probably began in August 1974, when parapsychologists Kerry Gaynor and Dr Barry Taff were studying the entity case of a woman called Doris Bither, who was allegedly being attacked and raped by unseen forces at 11547 Braddock Drive in Culver City, California. Her story inspired the popular 1982 horror movie *The Entity*.

The case was compelling because Bither, a single mother of four, was not alone in experiencing and witnessing the attacks – her children and others had too. It was also interesting because, during their lengthy investigation, Gaynor and Taff photographed on numerous occasions pops of strange three-dimensional light that were greenish-yellow and white in appearance. The orbs did not appear to be projected light, and Gaynor and Taff were at a loss to explain them. Taff did tentatively suggest it might have been possible for Bither's subconscious mind to generate enough energy to produce luminous anomalies and apparitions.

In contrast to this case, orbs are not typically seen with your eyes at the time the image is taken. Unexplained blurry images of orbs giving the appearance of rapid motion are one of the most popular but also controversial subjects within the field of paranormal investigation. More often than not orbs are noticed *after* the film is developed or the photographs are viewed. Paranormal experts suggest that the reason orbs can be viewed on film but not with the naked eye is due to the wider spectrum of ultraviolet light that film is sensitive to when compared to the human eye. Sceptics argue that the explanation is dust on the lens or a trick of the light, flaws in the camera, pixel fallout, infrared light waves reflecting particles in front of the lens, lens flare, reflections, plasma electricity, smoke, gas, human breath, tiny insects, water spots or deliberate fraud.

Although the great majority of orb sightings can be explained as non-paranormal, there is no denying that whenever a location is said to be haunted, images of orbs captured on film tend to cluster. Also, the sheer number of orbs you can view online suggests there are a lot of cameras out there that are flawed. Not to mention that orb images can be a source of tremendous comfort to the grieving, offering hope that a departed loved one is watching over them.

91. DEMONS AND ANGELS

There is always going to be debate as to the existence of ghosts, spirits, demons and the like. As this section has showcased, there are many people out there strongly committed to the belief that inhuman, evil entities do exist and can attach themselves to the vulnerable or to objects or places. And this belief shows no sign of ebbing away.

In 2022, a stretch of rural road located just outside Bath, England, which runs between Bathford and Farleigh Wick, suddenly emerged as yet another hot new contender for the world's most haunted location. 'Sally in the Wood', as this stretch of road is now called, was damaged by a landslide a few years ago. But some have suggested that the cracks in the road were not caused by nature but by something very sinister indeed – the spirit of a murdered girl torturing those who pass by. The unusual number of deaths and accidents on the road and the belief that birds never sing there have also been connected to the evil entity. There have also been reports of a girl in a white dress running into the road, causing a crash and then disappearing. During the English Civil War, the word 'sally' implied a sudden rush upon an enemy from a besieged place, and in this case it seems 'Sally' has intertwined with the sinister stories and tragic accidents that happened there.

Perhaps the most chilling thing about cases of inhuman or demonic possession are the personal accounts and sheer depth of the conviction of the believers. Even if the facts suggest otherwise, they are utterly convinced that what they experienced or witnessed was real. Do these kinds of encounters really happen? It is impossible to know, but it is important at the end of this section to point out that just as there is belief in evil spirits, there is also belief in good spirits. And belief is always a personal choice.

This category has focused on demonic hauntings because that is what most people think of when the words 'inhuman' and 'haunting' are used, but inhuman hauntings can of course also include angelic, animal and elemental hauntings.

Belief that elemental spirits – earth, fire, air and water – inhabit every living thing in nature is known as animism, believed to be the oldest spirituality in the world. Elementals go by countless different names, such as fairies, dragons, elves, nymphs, mermaids, trolls, pixies and leprechauns. They are the so-called spirits or consciousness or energy of trees, rivers, mountains and every natural living thing and are thought to be the cause of both natural disasters and blessings.

Animal ghost stories are also well documented. Some of these stories are alarming, such as the lore surrounding demonic hounds, but far outweighing this negativity are stories from pet owners who have sensed the loving presence of a departed pet. And in much the same way, although angels aren't typically thought of as hauntings because they are not sinister and don't typically trigger fear in the witness, belief in heavenly guides far outweighs belief in demons. Stories from people who believe angels protect, save and heal them are steadily on the increase, and some of these stories hit the headlines.

In 2008, an American lady called Colleen Banton talked to the press about her belief in miracles, and her story was widely reported in the media and remains online.

In brief, her fourteen-year-old daughter, Chelsea, who had a history of serious health issues, lay dying in a hospital room in Charlotte, North Carolina. Told by doctors there was no hope for her beloved daughter, Colleen agreed to life support being switched off. But then, as she watched her daughter fade away, a bright light, possibly in the shape of an angel, suddenly appeared on a nearby security monitor.

One hour later, doctors were at a loss to explain Chelsea's inexplicable recovery. Colleen was convinced that the bright light was an angel and that the angel saved her daughter's life. She took a photograph of the image on the monitor. Some who look at it say it is a flare of reflected light. Others, including on-duty nurses at the time, say the three vertical shafts of light are indisputably an angel.

Colleen's story is dramatic, but 'miracle' stories like hers are not the backbone of the current surge of belief in angels. Instead, it is the vast number of regular people from all walks of life who believe angels watch over them in ordinary but extraordinary ways that are giving angels a new lease of life.

These people may not see visions of angels with their eyes open, but they do see them in their dreams or in their mind's eye.

They sense them around. Some believe their departed loved ones become their guardian angels and send reassuring afterlife signs or calling cards, such as the unexpected appearance of a white feather or a robin or a butterfly. They also talk of sensing the loving and empowering presence of pure goodness.

But angels, their many disguises and the infinite comfort, love and joy belief in them can bring, is the subject of another book ...

INTELLIGENT

'An idea, like a ghost, must be spoken
to a little before it will explain itself.'

Anon, but credited to Charles Dickens

Of all the types of ghost story included in this book, intelligent, or intentional, hauntings are the category that has by far the most potential to truly advance our understanding of ghosts and hauntings, and it presents the very real possibility of life after death actually existing. For those who believe ghosts are spirits of the afterlife, this is the consciousness of someone who has died *intentionally* trying to react to or communicate or interact with the living.

The ten 'hauntings' gathered together here strongly suggest an intelligence or consciousness is at play, and in some cases such an encounter moved the experiencer so much that it led to a significant breakthrough in afterlife research. The previous three categories proposed that certain people can act as conscious or unconscious magnets for unexplained activity and certain buildings, objects and locations can also trigger reports of spooky encounters. However, in the case of intelligent hauntings, the clearest defining characteristic is that the initiative strongly appears to come not from the human witness but from the alleged ghost or spirit. The apparitions definitely want to be noticed and more often than not appear to consciously want to communicate with the living, often without invitation or warning.

Up close and personal

This interaction with the living can be initiated through a medium, but it can also happen directly to anyone without an intermediary raising the vibration or opening the lines of communication to the other side. The ghost may appear to people in their spirit form or communicate through a sense of presence, sounds, or a message in a dream or in afterlife signs (such as the random appearance of a white feather or a robin unexpectedly crossing your path) and other meaningful coincidences (synchronicity is the supernatural term). The encounters are typically spontaneous, unexpected, deeply personal and loaded with meaning for the experiencer alone. The experiencer does not require any validation because in their heart they now have all the 'proof' of an afterlife they need. As a result, apart from the word of the experiencer, their story is far less easy to research and record, hence the lower number of entries in this category.

We need to talk

Sometimes it appears as if ghosts actually want to 'talk' to the living. This can be through visions, dreams, voices and signs but also through the movement of physical objects. If you have ever watched the movie *Ghost*, starring Whoopi Goldberg as reluctant medium Oda May Brown, many mediums say this iconic movie, as well as being the first positive representation of a medium on screen, got some things right about the way spirits try to communicate with the living. The ghost, played by Patrick Swayze, has to learn to concentrate his spiritual energy – use the power of focused intention – to move a coin to convince his grieving widow, played by Demi Moore, that although he has died in this life, he is watching over and continuing to love her in the next.

In essence, ghosts may be as eager to learn ways to communicate effectively with us as we are with them.

92. RATTLING CHAINS

The earliest documented report of a haunting appears to be an intelligent haunting. It comes from a letter written by Pliny the Younger, a Roman orator (c. AD 113), to his patron, Lucas Sura. Pliny begins his letter: 'I am extremely desirous therefore to know whether you believe in the existence of ghosts, and that they have a real form, and are a sort of divinities, or only the visionary impressions of a terrified imagination.'

Pliny shares the story of a villa in Athens which is thought to be haunted and impossible to sell for that reason. At night the sounds of clanking chains are heard by terrified passers-by, and some have seen the apparition of an old, bearded man. Whoever lived in the villa soon moved out and put it up for sale again, hoping someone oblivious to its haunted history would move in.

Eventually, a brave philosopher named Athenodorus decided to move into the villa, intrigued by its low cost and the ghost attached to it. He decided he would sit up at night and wait for the ghost to appear in order to discover why it was so restless and unable to find peace in the afterlife. Right on cue, the ghost appeared to him in the dead of the night and rattled his chains around as if he was trying to point to something before vanishing.

Here again, in the words of Pliny:

> He looked up, saw, and recognized the ghost exactly as it had been described to him: it stood before him, beckoning with the finger, like a person who calls another. Athenodorus in reply made a sign with his hand that it should wait a little, and threw his eyes again upon his papers; the ghost then rattled its chains over the head of the philosopher, who looked up upon this, and seeing it beckoning as before, immediately arose, and, light in hand, followed it. The ghost slowly stalked along, as if encumbered with its chains, and, turning into the area of the house, suddenly vanished. Athenodorus, being thus deserted, made a mark with some grass and leaves on the spot where the spirit left him.
>
> The next day he gave information to the magistrates, and advised them to order that spot to be dug up. This was accordingly done, and the skeleton of a man in chains was found there; for the body, having lain a considerable time in the ground, was putrefied and mouldered away from the fetters. The bones being collected together were publicly buried, and thus after the ghost was appeased by the proper ceremonies, the house was haunted no more.

What is significant about this ancient ghost story is that all the people involved were highly educated, prominent men in Roman society – not likely candidates to make something like this up. It reads like a parable and the moral is clear: the ghost couldn't find peace in the afterlife until his death had been noticed by the living and his physical remains respected. Perhaps there's a lesson here about not automatically fearing ghosts, even if they appear utterly terrifying. They may need a little help and understanding from you to find their peace.

93. THE FOX SISTERS

Spiritualism is the belief that death ends a life, not a relationship, and that it is possible to communicate intelligently with spirits of the dead, especially through a medium or channel. Belief in communicating with the dead is age-old, but modern spiritualism is thought to have been born in Hydesville, New York State, on 31 March 1848, when two girls allegedly made contact with the afterlife.

Maggie and Kate Fox, aged fourteen and eleven, claimed to be in contact with spirits from the other side that communicated with them through loud raps on the wall and moving furniture. They would ask the entity to count to a certain number and it responded with the correct number of raps.

The sisters were sent to live with their older sister Leah in nearby Rochester, but the story of the ghost rapping followed them. Soon they were in demand for demonstrations, and in those demonstrations Leah discovered her mediumship abilities. Notable seer Andrew Jackson Davis was very impressed and lent the girls his full endorsement. The Fox sisters started to travel the country, and their demonstrations attracted huge crowds.

Sceptics did challenge them but were at a loss to explain the rapping, until 1888 when Maggie told an audience that it had been a childhood prank. The girls had used an apple tied to a piece of string to make the sounds, and they had also clicked their knuckles and toes. She claimed Leah had exploited her younger sisters. Despite this stunning confession, medium mania had by then well and truly gripped America and the world. Spiritualists remained convinced that communication with the other side through a medium was possible. A year later Maggie changed her story, saying that her spirit guides had confused her into a false confession – but although some believed her, the spiritualist movement as a whole turned its back on her.

Undaunted and spurred on by the initial success of the Fox sisters, hundreds of mediums started to come forward claiming they could communicate with the other side, and many of them gained a huge following. Around 1854, another pair of siblings from upstate New York, Ira and William Davenport, also claimed they had the ability to communicate with spirits. However, their demonstration, which included the infamous spirit cabinet illusion (a box in which mediums sat and were tied up before a curtain was closed and 'spirit signs' would appear, only for the medium to be revealed still tied up once the curtain was pulled back) had the feel of a magician's act and blurred the lines between entertainment and genuine attempts by mediums to communicate with the other side.

94. ELEMENTARY, MY DEPARTED!

Sir Arthur Conan Doyle is famous as the British author of the Sherlock Holmes detective stories. Less well known is that he was fascinated by the paranormal and is regarded as one of the founders of spiritualism. He joined the Society for Psychical Research and in 1883 founded the College of Psychic Studies, which is still in existence today in a South Kensington townhouse, where it continues to support psychic and mediumship abilities and research.

At the peak of his literary career, Doyle was so emboldened by his belief in a spirit world that he published two essays that firmly linked him to spiritualism: *The New Revelation* (1918) and *The Vital Message* (1919). However, his most seminal book on spiritualism is the two-volume *The History of Spiritualism* (1926). Doyle's critics suggest that he published this book because he was grief-stricken over the loss of his son Kingsley to pneumonia, but Doyle fiercely denied this. He stated that a year after his son's death he had visited a medium and believed she was the real deal, because she spoke in his son's voice and shared information it would be impossible for her to know.

Doyle was involved in a number of high-profile controversies. In July 1917, sixteen-year-old Elsie Wright and her ten-year-old cousin Frances Griffiths claimed to have seen and taken photographs of fairies in a small wooded creek behind Elsie's home in Cottingley, West Yorkshire. The picture shows Elsie with fairies allegedly dancing in front of her. Even though her parents were unconvinced, the girls gained a supporter in Doyle, who printed the images in a 1920 edition of *The Strand Magazine* and wrote a feature about them. He later expanded his feature into a book called *The Coming of the Fairies*. For decades the photos were deemed false, with even Doyle himself eventually admitting that may have been the case. It wasn't until long after his death that the truth finally came out in 1980. Frances and Elsie admitted they had faked the photographs as an act of revenge against their parents for telling them fairies were not real, and when Doyle got involved, they were so in awe of him they did not want to embarrass him. They also insisted they did actually see fairies as young girls but fairies don't like to be photographed.

In the 1920s, when Doyle was president of the London Spiritualist Alliance, a medium the alliance had approved of was charged with fortune telling – at the time illegal – and the alliance was fined £800. Doyle wrote a public protest in *The Times*, suggesting that this was persecution and urging that the Fortune Telling Act be modified or, better still, abolished. Six days before his death in July 1930, he led a petition to that effect.

One week after his death, a spiritual meeting was held in his honour and a chair left empty as a sign of respect. A medium claimed to see him sitting in the chair and offered messages to his family. Since then, many mediums have claimed to channel messages from the spirit of Sir Arthur Conan Doyle.

95. GO TO SLEEP, MARGARET

Although credit for the invention of the telephone is believed to lie with Alexander Graham Bell, who patented the first telephone in 1876, inventor Thomas Edison played a vital part in 1877 when he invented the carbon microphone, which produced a strong telephone signal. He also invented the 'talking machine', aka the phonograph or gramophone, the first record player to record and play back sound.

Edison spent decades perfecting his talking machine and other visionary inventions, including his 1880 patent for an electric lamp that would eventually pave the way for the universal use of electric light bulbs. What you may not know, however, is that about a decade before his death in 1931, he announced that he was working on a new machine that he believed could enable people to talk to the dead and also record messages from the dead to the living.

Edison was convinced that science, rather than a Ouija board or tilting table, was the way forward. He described mediumship as 'unscientific nonsense'. He believed that spirit energy was extremely sensitive and needed highly responsive equipment to pick it up. However, despite working patiently and diligently on it in his laboratory and holding an unsuccessful demonstration involving a lamp and a photo-electric cell in front of his peers, he was unable to prove that science could form a living connection with the afterlife.

Over the years, many people have, like Edison, attempted to use electrical devices or technology to connect to or record the other side. Electronic voice phenomena (EVP) is a case in point. From the 1960s onward, EVP became a popular method for ghost hunters to offer 'proof', and this remains the case today. It is simply leaving a recording device on and then listening to detect any unexplained sounds or voices that can only be heard when the tape is played back or amplified with noise filtering. The problem with EVP records is the natural human tendency to project meaning on or find patterns in sounds that are random or innocent.

The quality of recordings varies greatly, but there are some standout ones that appear to suggest intelligent communication, such as recordings by Latvian intellectual Konstantīns Raudive, discussed in his 1971 book *Breakthrough: An Amazing Experiment in Electronic Communication with the Dead*. Raudive stated that he had heard many voices in German, French and Latvian when he had first started experimenting with EVP and one of them said, 'Go to sleep, Margaret.' This impressed him greatly, as he had recently lost someone dear called Margaret, and it encouraged him to spend the next decade researching EVP with hundreds of experts and witnesses under 'strict laboratory conditions'.

Edison's original quest to offer evidence in this electronic area continues to this day. Anomalous telephone communication was researched seriously in *Phone Calls from the Dead*, a 1979 book written by American paranormal experts D. Scott Rogo and Raymond Bayless, and in a 2012 book entitled *Telephone Calls from the Dead*, parapsychologist Dr Callum E. Cooper continued the research they had started. University of Arizona psychologist Gary Schwartz is actively working with engineers to pioneer soul phone technology to prove it is possible to communicate with the other side. Today, the general consensus on EVP among paranormal enthusiasts is that it could offer proof of ghosts attempting to communicate with us, but many scientists continue to think of EVP as auditory pareidolia, which is recognizing patterns and/or words in random sounds.

96. THE SETH MATERIAL

A number of visionaries have claimed that their work was 'channelled' by a higher spiritual power, as have a number of spiritual thought leaders, such as Jane Roberts. Born in the 1920s in New York, Roberts allegedly channelled a vast body of written material that may well have inspired the so-called New Age Movement. In 1963, Roberts was writing poetry at her desk and felt an 'avalanche' of creative ideas explode in her head. She believed a spirit guide called Seth – 'an energy presence no longer focused in physical matter' – was using her body to speak through her, calling her to write down his teachings.

The Seth Material was published in 1969 and claims to be a direct dictation from the spirit of Seth. It contains many ideas which define the New Age Movement today, including the theory that consciousness creates reality and that the power of thought and expectation can transform lives. In essence, it was a manual for the power of positive feeling, or manifesting. Roberts died in 1984, and right until the end she insisted she was simply the conduit. Throughout her life her output was prolific, with ten volumes of Seth books.

It could be said that channelling is simply tuning into your intuition and creativity and that anyone who has ever lost track of time when in a state of flow or immersed in a task is channelling. But there are those that believe channelling is not of human origin; it is a direct connection to the invisible psychic world or some awareness greater than your own.

Jane Roberts was not the first and will by no means be the last person to claim that out-of-this-world wisdom was 'channelled' through her by a spiritual being or entity. Countless people have used that word to elevate their art, their writing or their message to something akin to divine inspiration. Esther Hicks, an American inspirational speaker, channeller and author, along with her husband Jerry, is an influential example. Esther presented the New Thought Movement mantra of the law of attraction, which inspired million-copy-selling *The Secret* by Rhonda Byrne and the current manifesting self-help trend, endorsed by the likes of Oprah, Lady Gaga and Will Smith. Esther has claimed her message and her books were 'translated from a group of non-physical entities called Abraham'. She describes what she is doing as tapping into 'infinite intelligence'.

97. THE MEDIUM WHISPERERS

Julie Beischel holds a PhD in Pharmacology and Toxicology with a minor in Microbiology and Immunology from the University of Arizona. In 2017, along with her husband Mark Boccuzzi, she founded the Windbridge Research Center, which carries out research into mediumship and publishes groundbreaking research.

The story behind Beischel's decision to forfeit a traditional academic path, and most probably a career working for a pharmaceutical company, occurred following her mother's death. As she went through the grieving process, she decided to visit a medium.

The reading included information it was impossible for the medium to know – in particular specific details about her mother's death by suicide, as well as insight she didn't know at the time but which was later confirmed by members of her extended family. It convinced her that something she could not explain had happened, and when other academics she knew all claimed that mediums were con artists, she decided to break the mould and use her interdisciplinary training to study afterlife communication with scientific rigour.

Windbridge has studied mediums' psychology, physiology, business practices, demographics and experiences and published peer-reviewed journal articles and anthology chapters discussing these factors and the potential therapeutic application of mediumship readings during bereavement.

One groundbreaking study, published by Windbridge and IONS (the Institute of Noetic Sciences), involved fifty-eight readings with twenty mediums and provides perhaps the strongest evidence yet for anomalous information reception by volunteer mediums. The accuracy reported by mediums during phone readings performed under controlled, blind laboratory conditions that address alternative explanations such as fraud, cueing, cold reading and generalizations was way above chance.

IONS, like Windbridge, also actively researches afterlife communication under strict laboratory conditions. A team of highly respected scientists there are currently leading the world in consciousness research. Their studies show that paranormal experiences at the very least deserve credible scientific investigation, because people have been having these experiences since the beginning of time and continue to do so. All these stories need to be treated as data, and what the team at IONS are finding is that when studied scientifically, in the majority of cases there is reason to believe the explanation could be paranormal. For example, studies where mediums are given photographs of people and asked to classify their cause of death show that the mediums score above chance in accuracy.

Today, a number of highly respected universities and institutions have dedicated parapsychology units and/or laboratories where afterlife communication and psychic ability is researched as a social science and/or tested as an ability people naturally have and which they can learn to awaken and develop. For instance, the Koestler Parapsychology Unit at the University of Edinburgh; the centre for the study of anomalous psychological phenomena at the University of Northampton; the Division of Perceptual Studies at the University of Virginia; the parapsychology laboratory of Duke University in Durham, North Carolina; and the parapsychology research unit at the University of Arizona. Tried and tested scientific procedures are used in these research units, of which the Ganzfeld Protocol, which completely limits external and sensory input when testing for psychic abilities, is best known.

Not forgetting that some brilliant Nobel Peace Prize-winning scientists, past and present (such as Professor Brian Josephson, Alan Turing, Max Planck and Wolfgang Pauli), have been very open-minded about the paranormal and the possibility of there being life after death. However, despite this, there is no denying that definitive proof of the afterlife – and therefore of ghosts and spirits – just isn't there yet. The important thing, though, is that progress *is* being made by credible academic researchers all over the world. You might want to follow that research or, better still, volunteer to be a part of it, as there is no telling what it may uncover.

98. A PARTING VISION

Visions of departed loved ones appearing and communicating to a dying person a few days, hours or sometimes moments before their death are more common than you might think. These deeply personal stories are always best told by the people they happened to or by the people who actually witnessed them happening. Joseph sent me his story:

> Mercifully, my wife died in her sleep and there was no pain or stress. I was with her at the end, and before she shut her eyes for the last time she commented that her room felt crowded. I didn't understand so I just squeezed her hand tight to reassure her I was there. She then told me her mother and father and her best friend Sally were all sitting at the bottom of her bed. She thanked me for bringing them to her. I was confused as both her parents were long dead and her friend Sally had passed ten years ago. I put it down to exhaustion and mental confusion and just sat quietly listening.
>
> For the next few minutes my wife 'talked' to her parents and to Sally. She asked them questions and I could see her nod and react as if they were replying. It was surreal, witnessing this invisible communication. Eventually, my wife turned to me and said her parents wanted her to sleep now and would tuck her in now and sit with her till she fell asleep. She said it was fine for me to go now. I kissed her on the cheek and sat back in my chair.
>
> The last memory I have of my wife alive is her falling asleep with a hint of a smile on her face, like a contented child tucked in by loving parents.

Sceptics are quick to point out that parting visions may be a kind of natural sedative released in the brain to ease the fear of dying, or the result of medication or hallucinations, but even if this is the case, it can't fully explain the strength and peace they bring not just to the dying but to their loved ones. It also can't fully explain why lots of reports of deathbed visions don't come from the person dying, or even from loved ones present at the scene, but from medical staff and hospice workers. These people obviously have a duty of care, and although they are no doubt highly empathetic, they would not have the same intense emotional bond that family members and friends would experience.

Jac, a hospice worker with over three decades of experience caring for the terminally ill, sent me this story:

In my line of work death is a way of life.

One afternoon as I was coming in to check on a lady called Judith who never had any visitors, she grabbed my hand and told me that I didn't need to sit with her anymore because they were with her now. I asked her what she meant and she said her siblings. She came from a family of eight and all had passed before her. Then she touched my face and thanked me. It was the first sign of tenderness I had ever known from her.

A few days later I sat with Judith as she passed peacefully in her sleep.

This was not an isolated incident and I have witnessed things similar over the decades. I don't ask to see what I see, but it happens. It is beautiful.

99. WHAT DREAMS MAY COME

Visions of departed loved ones are rare, but they can and do happen. Over the years I have received many true stories, like this one sent to me by Leah:

> I was working from home and suddenly felt very sleepy so I decided to take a nap. When I woke up my mum was standing in front of me. She had a spare key so I didn't think anything of it. She gave me a kiss and told me she loved me but couldn't stop and chat as she had lots to do and we would catch up later. My mum was one of these people who are always rushing from one thing to another so this seemed perfectly normal. I went back to work.
>
> About five minutes later the telephone rang. It was my brother and he was crying. He told me that my mother had had a stroke and had passed away on the way to hospital. I told him that was impossible as I had literally just seen her in my flat. My brother told me I must be mistaken or dreaming as my mother had been at home when she had her stroke and he had called the ambulance. I really don't know if I was dreaming or not and I can't believe it happened to me as I am not spiritual. All I know is that I saw my mother and I believe she was saying goodbye.

I have no reason to doubt anyone who writes to me, especially as many people express surprise that something like this happened. They often say they find it hard to believe it happened themselves – but happen it did. They were not dreaming or imagining it.

Leah does mention she had woken up from a short nap, and many visions of departed loved ones do occur in that twilight state between waking and sleeping. But Leah remains convinced she was wide awake at the time. From all my research, whether a vision of a departed person is seen with eyes closed or open, or whether it appears solid and real or elusive, in virtually all cases the impact is empowering. The observer is left with a feeling that their loved one is somehow alive in spirit. Research into bereavement and afterlife dreams led by Dr Callum E. Cooper at the University of Northampton confirms that in at least 85 per cent of cases, those who experience afterlife dreams are better able to manage their grief. This is something I already knew from the afterlife dream stories sent to me by my readers and which I have experienced for myself.

100. SIGNS

Afterlife signs, or calling cards, are believed to be direct personal communications with the afterlife without visiting a medium. They can offer wonderful reassurance that relationships can continue in spirit. They are typically spontaneous, gentle and subtle. Here is an example, sent to me by Russell:

> It was the morning of my GCSE maths examination and I was super nervous. I had worked very hard but I had missed a lot of school in recent months due to a serious chest infection. I had done my best to catch up but my confidence was low. I wanted to get a good enough grade for university so the exam was important. It was not my strongest subject though, as I lean more towards the arts and I knew it, as did my teachers.

Anyway, on the morning of the exam after eating my breakfast and [while] my mother was tidying everything, I had a panic attack. I started to sweat and feel faint and sick. My mother felt my head and it was hot and we debated ducking out of the exam when suddenly I heard, 'The force is with you, young Skywalker,' boom out from my *Star Wars* mug sitting on the windowsill, which had a battery-operated voice pack. We burst out laughing and all my nerves vanished.

I got that mug six years ago when I was deep in my *Star Wars* phase. It had been a gift from my dad who had died the year afterwards from cancer leaving my mother and me to cope alone. Dad and I shared a love for *Star Wars* but after he died I stopped watching all the movies. It was too painful. Every time you lifted the mug up it would say, 'The force is with you,' and play the *Star Wars* theme tune. The batteries had died years ago and I couldn't face it being in my bedroom but I couldn't throw it away because it was the last gift my dad gave me before he got really ill, so it had languished on the kitchen windowsill.

My mother said it was the sunlight that triggered the speaker but the batteries were dead and it had never happened before and has not happened since. I believe it was my father in spirit trying to give me a bout of humour and self-belief. It worked. I passed my exam and am at university now. I have had other signs from my dad as well as dreams of him. I feel his presence with me all the time. Forgive the pun but I know his force is forever alive within me!

To date, this is perhaps the only 'the afterlife spoke to me through *Star Wars*' story sent to me, and I am showcasing it here to illustrate that it is impossible to generalize about afterlife signs. They are deeply personal experiences and can be anything meaningful to you. The common theme is that you just know a departed loved one is close by and it brings tremendous comfort.

However, although I have said anything can be a potential spiritual sign, I have found that from the many stories sent to me over the years, some signs are more common or more likely to occur than others, and these include: white feathers appearing in unexpected places; finding coins with significant dates; invisible sensations, such as a kiss; mysterious scents that remind you of a loved one; appliances playing up (lights flickering, clocks stopping); music (hearing a meaningful song at just the right time); objects lost and found; a spontaneous sense or feeling that your loved one is close by; nature signs, like clouds and rainbows; repeating numbers; coincidences; birds and animals behaving in unusual ways; and, last but by no means least, afterlife dreams.

101. YOU

Reading true afterlife stories is a way to honour the past and remember the lessons learned from history. It is also an undying reminder that however bizarre the stories appear, they always have a human origin. At some point someone either experienced, witnessed or believed in the possibility of the paranormal, and over time that possibility gathered a death-defying life of its own. And that someone was a human being just like you.

Research suggests that some people may be more sensitive

than others and therefore more likely to experience ghosts and hauntings. But whether you identify as highly sensitive or not, or are inclined to believe in an afterlife or not, this final entry is a reminder that every person who has ever lived is haunted not just by history but by their own ghosts.

Every person lives with memories of departed loved ones. It is often said that people die twice: first when they die physically, and second when they are not remembered by anyone. So carrying the memories of departed loved ones in our minds and hearts is a way to keep them alive and with us always.

And that includes you.

As this book has been keen to stress repeatedly, ghostly places and encounters are a natural part of the human experience – the norm and not the exception. Unexplained experiences are simply aspects of our existence that we need to understand better. Instead of fearing or dismissing the uncanny, get excited about their mystery, as they suggest there is more to you and this life than meets the eye. And if you have ever dreamt of a departed loved one, or noticed meaningful afterlife signs, or lost yourself in loving memories, or inexplicably sensed you are not alone in the darkness, then let yourself wonder if in that moment the veil between this life and the next has lifted.

You have no idea why or how, but perhaps part of you senses that those you have loved and lost are never far away and you are not alone.

CONCLUSION: THE NEVER-ENDING GHOST STORY

'Tis the middle of night by the castle clock,
And the owls have awakened the crowing cock;
Tu—whit!—Tu—whoo!
And hark, again! the crowing cock,
How drowsily it crew.'

'Christabel',
Samuel Taylor Coleridge

As long as humans walk the earth, their ghosts will walk beside them. I hope the entries in this book have given you a tantalizing glimpse of our never-ending love story with ghosts. And glimpse is the perfect word here, because as substantial as it may seem, all you have digested so far is really just offering you a hint of your haunted world.

The biggest challenge when writing this book was deciding what to include; given the vast number of possible entries, one book was never going to be enough to include them all. The choice of entries is personal and chosen to reveal the bigger picture, giving you a snapshot in the hope it will whet your appetite to discover more for yourself. And there is always infinitely more for you to discover when you start investigating this haunted world.

HALLOWEEN

I couldn't write a book on hauntings without mentioning the Day of the Dead, celebrated in Mexico between 31 October and 2 November, and, of course, Halloween, also known as All Hallows' Eve or Samhain. Celebrated on 31 October, Halloween is traditionally associated with an increased risk of hauntings – but none of the stories in this book reference it (or even that dread combination of Friday and the number 13), proving that paranormal activity really isn't reserved for a specific day of the year alone. It can happen on any day at any time, all year round. And for those who believe in an afterlife, every day is Halloween.

The simple reason there tends to be more interest in ghost stories at Halloween is because of a shared belief that Halloween is the day for ghosts to come out and party. What you focus on is what you notice, and on Halloween, collective attention is on the possibility of ghosts. Halloween is quite literally Christmas Day for ghost-hunting tours and campfire storytellers. There are also dramatic increases in ghost investigations and eyewitness reports of paranormal activity.

And that collective belief has an ancient history. The festival traces its origins back to pagan times, when the ancient Celts celebrated the end of summer, days becoming shorter and their belief that on that day, the veil between the living and the dead was at its thinnest and the dead could rise out of their graves to wander freely on the earth. The living would dress up as ghosts so that spirits would not be able to recognize them, and huge bonfires would be lit in an attempt to rekindle the diminishing energy of the sun god in the winter. The ancient Romans also celebrated festivals, such as the festival of Pomona, the goddess of harvest, that influenced Halloween traditions involving pumpkins and apples. And over time fairies, witches and goblins as well as ghosts and spirits were also said to flourish on Halloween night.

Today, the tradition of Halloween is enjoying new-found popularity. This isn't just in America – where Halloween has been an established part of American folklore since the 1840s, when many Irish people fled to the United States and brought their traditions with them – but in the UK and Europe too. For modern-day wiccans and pagans, All Hallows' Eve is one of their most sacred days and a time to honour the dead and find light in the darkness. And for ghost hunters it is when the night light shines most brightly on them.

GHOST HUNTERS

Modern ghost hunters often use technology and high-tech equipment in their investigation of alleged hauntings, in contrast to their nineteenth-century predecessors, who had no choice but to rely on anecdotal accounts, photographs and their own intuitive and observational skills. Among the first to pioneer the use of technology in a ghost investigation was London-born psychical researcher Harry Price, one of the most highly influential and colourful figures in the history of ghost hunting. In his 1926 to 1938 investigation of an alleged haunting at Borley Rectory (see page 90), he installed a paranormal research lab which included cameras, fingerprinting equipment, recorders, a telescope and a telephone. Despite this he was criticized by his peers for his flamboyant manner, his love of entertaining an audience and, most of all, his lack of scientific training.

These days, ghost hunting has increasingly become highly sophisticated and scientific in its approach. There is a whole world of ghost-hunting experts out there. Some of these, such as American parapsychologist Loyd Auerbach (aka Professor Paranormal), work alongside scientific research centres like the Rhine Research Center. Dr Chris Roe, Professor in Parapsychology, and Dr Callum E. Cooper, from the University of Northampton, conduct ghost investigations and research alleged paranormal activity in a highly professional and academic way, utilizing high-tech equipment whenever appropriate. Sometimes, as is the case for Loyd Auerbach, private individuals who believe their home is haunted may contact him directly to conduct a thorough investigation. The aim of such studies is to rule out all logical or natural explanations, and on the rare occasion this can't be done, it is to research the history of the house and its current residents to find out why the energy may be unsettling and a potential magnet for mysterious things happening. Most important of all, the goal is to offer reassurance that can help people lose their fear.

However, alongside professional ghost hunters with serious research credentials behind them, it is important to note that there is an ever-increasing army of amateur ghost hunters out there too. Every day, all over the world, ghost hunts take place. Some of these are presented as entertainment, such as overnight vigils organized at locations which have become famous for their resident ghosts, whereas others may take place in local restaurants, pubs, parks or ordinary homes.

The use of technology in both amateur and professional ghost hunts has dramatically transformed the nature and scope of paranormal investigation. Although this technology can detect temperature shifts and noise vibrations and capture on film what might otherwise be invisible to the human eye, some ghost-hunting enthusiasts feel it can become a distraction and may rob the investigation of its mystery. (Not to mention that such equipment is often very expensive, limiting the opportunity for low-income, would-be researchers to get hold of it.) However, others believe that relying purely on a ghost hunter's intuition and/or an on-site medium, as well as anecdotal accounts or eyewitness statements, is deeply flawed, as it can never successfully rule out the power of suggestion or telepathy and, most important of all, accusations of mentalism and trickery.

Mentalism is a kind of mystery entertainment or modern stage magic where the five senses are used to create the illusion of a sixth sense at work. It is brilliantly showcased today by the likes of the mesmerizing British mentalist Derren Brown and American illusionist David Copperfield. Some mentalists use their skills to show people how easily fraudulent psychics and mediums can make it seem as if they truly are reading minds or talking to dead people.

The use of ghost-hunting equipment remains controversial, but there is no doubt it can be used to rule out the possibility of mentalism and fraud, which virtually every entry in this book will find levelled at it by sceptics. It also enables ghost hunters to collect data and record paranormal activity with time and date stamps over an extended period of time. Sometimes this data can be collected without the ghost hunter even having to visit the site.

There is a long way to go yet before we have definitive proof of there being life after death, but if/when that proof comes, in my humble opinion it is highly likely that high-tech ghost-hunting equipment will be present or at the forefront of it.

GHOST-HUNTING SURVIVAL TIPS

Whether you realize it or not, the fact that you were drawn to this book makes you an ideal candidate to become a ghost hunter because you have curiosity and an open mind.

Ghost hunters go to locations that are said to be haunted to try to capture evidence on camera or record sounds or experience something with their own eyes. Ghost hunting is by its nature exciting. You never know who or what you might stumble across and whether you are going to be the one who can actually offer proof of survival after death.

Of course, certain skills are required, and you can go on a number of in-person or online paranormal courses or join a ghost-hunting club to learn these. But don't let yourself get bogged down with jargon or think that someone else knows more about ghosts than you do.

When it comes to ghosts, we are all equally in the dark. Ghost hunting is not an exact science and there are always going to be different schools of thought, but the survival tips below will give you a firm foundation and see you safely and clearly through the night.

Know where to look

Cemeteries, hospitals, old buildings, museums, sacred/historical sites and hotels often inherit a wealth of ghost stories. But as this book has shown, ghosts can be reported anywhere and at any time, so wherever you are, it's always worth carrying a notebook with you, or a voice recorder so you can instantly document anything potentially out of this world.

Research

Before visiting the site, do as much research as possible. Dig deep for any information you can find so you are already an expert about any alleged hauntings before you arrive. If you can, you might want to interview eyewitnesses. And from this moment on, keep a record of all the facts and accounts you gather.

Teamwork

You may prefer to work alone, but for your safety and for your investigation to be taken seriously, it's a good idea to join a local ghost-hunting group or ask some like-minded people to join you.

Prepare

No smoking, drugs or alcohol during the ghost hunt for obvious reasons, and don't wear perfume or anything with a strong scent. If the place is open to the public, make sure you get permission to take photographs, and if it is private property, get permission to enter from the owners or residents first. If you are going to investigate at night, be sure to check out the area in daylight first so you are familiar with it and can avoid dangerous places and obstacles.

Tools

Make sure you have your essential ghost-hunting tools to capture potential evidence. These should include your ID in case you are questioned by anyone so you can prove who you are, a reliable digital camera, a torch, and an audio and video recording device with a time and date stamp. You may also want to bring a compass to detect potential magnetic fields, chalk to mark areas, binoculars, thermometers to detect temperature changes, motion detectors to sense unseen movement, and measuring tape to mark or measure areas. Of course, if you are going to investigate for several hours, make sure you wear appropriate clothing and bring food and drink along.

Paranormal investigation is similar to ghost hunting but goes into much greater depth and often involves an all-night vigil and the use of a medium. High-tech equipment, such as night-vision cameras, spotlights, headset communicators for a team, electromagnetic field meters to measure and locate potential sources of electromagnetism, thermal scanners, air ion counters and so on, may also be used, because the aim is to prove (or disprove) a haunting. It's a bit like an expensive forensic investigation of a crime scene, and if this is the case, it is probably best left to the experts and those with the funds to do this.

Ghost hunting, on the other hand, is something you can most certainly do yourself, as all you are trying to do is capture the atmosphere. Simply arrive at the scene and be as observant as possible. Keep your video camera recording throughout and dictate or write notes to yourself about any feelings or emotions you experience. Make sure your camera lens is free of dust and notice any light sources so when you review your footage you won't mistake a car light for an orb, for instance. The same applies for reflective shiny surfaces. If you are outdoors and it is cold or you are drinking something hot, be mindful of your breath.

LIGHTS ON

Keep an open mind during your ghost hunt and don't come to any conclusions or be influenced by the opinions of witnesses, owners or anyone else until you have had a chance to rewatch your video footage, listen to your voice notes and make up your own mind. And when making your mind up, be as logical and as sceptical as possible. Always, always rule out natural and rational explanations first. If you do end up with something which just can't be explained, you want to make sure it can withstand the inevitable scrutiny.

And if you get scared during your ghost hunt, or even when reading this book, that's OK. Fear is a natural human response, and there is no telling how you will react to the atmosphere of a location. The secret is to stay calm and simply record those moments of fear, but if you do feel overwhelmed, it is best to leave the scene behind you until you feel centred again. And a reminder that throughout the centuries, the living have repeatedly and consistently shown themselves to be far more terrifying than the dead!

Fear of what evil lurks in the darkness is ingrained. It goes right back to ancient times, when the impenetrability of night was the most vulnerable time for potential attack by animals, snakes or rival tribes. It also probably goes back to childhood, when your parents or carers bid you good night and switched off the lights. You were suddenly all alone with just your imagination to magnify sounds and shadows into something scary. In essence, it is perfectly natural to feel vulnerable in the dark, but it goes deeper than survival instinct or childhood separation anxiety – it is a nightly reminder that life is a balance between day and night, and there is a shadow within us all.

The ability to feel comfortable alone in the darkness is a giant and transformative leap of faith. It is facing your own shadow.

Understanding (but not indulging) your fears is how you grow in self-awareness. It is feeling at peace in your own company and knowing deep down that fear doesn't just happen to you. The threat isn't outside of you. It is an inner choice you make. You can choose calm instead.

Above all, darkness reminds us of our mortality. Death comes to us all, and fear of that final sleep is understandable, because death is still the great unknown. But feeling scared is a sign you are truly alive. And it is in the unknown, getting comfortable outside your comfort zone, that all progress happens. In short, transform your fear into excitement, because this perspective shift will help you understand that what you truly fear isn't death but dying with regrets. Ensure your days and your nights are memorable ones so that when your time comes, those regrets aren't there and death is simply the next great adventure.

WORKING WITH MEDIUMS?

Some ghost hunters and paranormal investigators prefer not to work with mediums and psychics or use tools such as Ouija boards or seances. Their argument is that mediumship and psychic ability is unscientific. Also, psychics and mediums are by their nature going to be biased towards belief in an afterlife. Shifting their focus from the spiritual and symbolic to the rational and literal may not be easy, and you will end up with a lot of vague and highly suggestive material that isn't all that helpful.

There are positives to working with mediums and psychics, because sometimes they can sense something intuitively that others may not be able to. The best mediums and psychics are ones that are humble and open to having their perspective questioned.

There are honest mediums out there who are sincere in their belief that they really can connect with the other side in a loving way. If you do want to work with a medium or a psychic, my suggestion is to work with ones who have been tested or certified in some way. For example, the Windbridge Institute (see page 254) requires a medium to undergo testing before they are certified, and the Forever Family Foundation also has criteria for its approved mediums. If a medium isn't certified, look at their training. There are mediumship training programmes run by respected establishments like the Arthur Findley College and the College of Psychic Studies in the UK. If the medium's background is obscure or celebrity, social media or TV endorsed – or based around a bestselling book – steer clear, especially if they have gathered a cult-like following.

Ultimately, trust your intuition, as some untrained mediums are sincere, often working without charge at spiritualist churches or psychic fairs because it is their vocation. Keep your sceptical hat on and avoid a medium or psychic who charges high fees (the price of a good haircut for a reading is a good marker), bombards you with advertising and requests for repeat visits or, most important of all, does not have a code of ethics or a willingness to consider other viewpoints apart from their own.

Sadly, fraud is too often the case, and bringing in a medium or psychic on a ghost hunt may well undermine your own perception. Indeed, what you yourself see, feel, hear, smell and sense is perhaps the most important consideration for every ghost hunter or paranormal expert.

Direct personal experience – your own perception and intuition – is always the best marker. One brilliant study underlines my position here. From 2018 to 2020, Dr Arnaud Delorme from IONS (see page 255) conducted a study of twelve volunteer mediums and twelve volunteer non-mediums or controls. Photos were given to all twenty-four participants and they were asked to determine cause of death just by looking at a photo. Intriguingly, the non-medium group outperformed the medium group. The mediums were nervous in the laboratory conditions, because when asked to repeat a similar experiment at home, their results improved. This study does not suggest mediums don't have mediumistic capability but it does imply that we all have such abilities and the reason the non-mediums did better was because they were not suffering from performance anxiety as the mediums were.

The moral of all this is that forcing or straining for results can create intuitive blocks, not just on a ghost hunt but in all areas of life. The best ghost story is one that you uncover for yourself, and I sincerely hope you will send me your haunting tales (details on how to do so can be found on page 281) and become a citizen parapsychologist in the process.

If we are ever to discover whether ghosts are real or not, my suspicion is that the truth will emerge not just via the science lab and high-tech equipment but also from collating the data they are the true stories of ordinary people, like you and me, who believe as they have experienced or witnessed something baffling.

SILENT FOOTSTEPS

Most of the time, ghosts manifest in what is felt or sensed but unseen – in memories and in vivid dreams or through deeply meaningful afterlife signs and synchronicities or the comforting feeling that you are not alone. In those blissful moments, you intuitively sense from the inside out a direct connection to the afterlife or something greater than yourself.

However, as the stories in this book have shown, sometimes ghosts appear more tangible. They seem willing and able to move from the world of shadows, and those invisible footsteps that have always been walking beside us seem to appear in the physical world. For a few tantalizing moments, when the circumstances are right, something unexplained is glimpsed, strange whispers are fleetingly heard, uncanny things that defy all attempts at natural explanation are recalled, felt, dreamt.

And along with all the other questions that battle for your attention, there is always one that lingers, perhaps more profoundly than others.

Was that a ghost?

The very real possibility that it could be, and the fact that this possibility can't be definitively ruled out in every single reported case, is a goosebump moment and more than enough to send shivers, perhaps not of fear and dread but of excitement and anticipation, down any spine!

AFTERWORD BY
G. L. DAVIES

I was introduced to ghost stories as a young boy.

I was enthralled and captivated by these paranormal encounters. It was so commonplace for those around me to discuss supernatural tales that I believed these were just a familiar part of our world. I was instantly enamoured with the topic, to the degree that I became that spooky kid who would bring Arthur C. Clarke's *Mysterious World and Photographs of the Unknown* to school with me to captivate and terrify my fellow pupils in equal measure.

Haunted World: 101 Ghostly Encounters by Theresa Cheung is a book I wish I had had at that age. I would have devoured each entry, imagining in great detail the places, the people and the ghosts that haunt its pages. Most surprising of all, perhaps, is that the stories here will fascinate not only those interested in the spooky things that creep in the shadows but also those interested in the history of their local area, for some will be shocked to know that such perplexing experiences have occurred just down the road in their quiet town or county.

People have asked what I define myself as – a paranormal investigator or a researcher. My answer is that I specialize in interviewing those with paranormal experiences and sharing these testimonies with the world. I have listened to and collected ghost stories for nearly forty years, and my offerings of *Haunted: Horror of Haverfordwest* and *Harvest: The True Story of Alien Abduction* are my attempts to give these witnesses a voice and keep the ancient tradition of sharing paranormal experiences alive.

Haunted World is a tremendous contribution to that effort. It is a book that avid enthusiasts will read, study and discuss as its collection of stories of otherworldly experiences guides them in their quest to pull back the veil and shine a light into the unknown. To be read in the dimming light as the stormy nights draw in, this book will inspire a whole new generation of paranormal researchers, enthusiasts and investigators, as well as those simply looking to be spooked as the temperature drops and the evenings grow darker.

And as you go forward with a heightened awareness of the things we don't yet understand, be sure to keep *Haunted World* close at hand. Maybe one day your own ghostly encounter will be featured in such a book.

Sleep well,
G. L. Davies

SUBMIT YOUR HAUNTING TALES

For the past thirty years I have been collating afterlife stories from my readers. As well as sharing some of these stories in my books and on my *White Shores* podcast, I also collaborate with scientists and parapsychologists researching the afterlife, and your stories are important data for their research. If shared, all names and other personal details are changed to protect identities.

So if you have a question or insight to share or a true ghost or haunting story and would like my feedback or advice, feel free to get in touch via the Contact Me page on my website, www.theresacheung.com. You can also message me via Instagram @thetheresacheung or my Facebook and X/Twitter author pages. Depending on how busy things get – and especially around Halloween – it may take a while for me to reply, but I aim to reply to everyone in due course. Hearing from my readers and listeners is what I love most about being a psychic world author.

ABOUT THE AUTHOR

Theresa Cheung is a *Sunday Times* bestselling supernormal author. She has a degree from King's College Cambridge University and is the author of numerous titles which have been translated into over forty different languages, including *The Dream Dictionary A to Z*, *The Element Encyclopedia of the Psychic World*, *The Element Encyclopedia of Ghosts and Hauntings* (Harper Collins) and *The Afterlife Is Real* (Schuster).

Theresa works closely with scientists and parapsychologists and has contributed features about the psychic world and the afterlife to newspapers and magazines, such as Bustle, *Vice*, *Cosmopolitan*, *Women's Health*, *OMTimes*, Refinery29, *InStyle*, *Good Housekeeping*, *Red*, *Heat*, *Glamour* and many more. A returning paranormal expert guest on ITV's *This Morning*, she has also been interviewed by Claudia Winkleman on BBC Radio 2, Roman Kemp on Capital Radio, Nicky Campbell on BBC 5 Live Sounds podcast *Different*, Regina Meredith on Gaia TV, George Noory on Coast to Coast, and on other leading media outlets including KTLA, Good Day Chicago, Today Extra, GMTV and Channel 4. A frequently requested guest on numerous celebrity podcasts, she is listed among the 100 most spiritually influential living people in *Watkins Mind Body Spirit* magazine and has given talks and webinars for leading companies and brands such as Beauty Bay, Anthropologie, Shiseido, Dynavision, Immediate Media, The Shift Network and the Hearst Magazine group. She also hosts her own popular podcast, *White Shores*.

You can follow and message Theresa on Instagram @thetheresacheung or via her Facebook and X/Twitter author pages and learn more about her work at www.theresacheung.com

ACKNOWLEDGEMENTS

I am deeply grateful to my editor, Jo Stansall, for the ghostly genesis and creepy creation of this book and for making it tremendous fun to work on. I would also like to thank Lucy Stewardson for her outstanding editing, spooky insight and literary flourish, as well as Catherine Dunn for her clear-eyed vision at copy-edit stage and everyone at Michael O'Mara Books involved in editing and production. Special gratitude to Alessandro Valdrighi for his mesmerizing and hauntingly evocative artwork. Thank you to Loyd Auerbach and G. L. Davies for their foreword and afterword, and to Gail Torr from Galaxy Media for being a paranormal powerhouse.

This book would not be possible without the tireless research of parapsychologists and scientists as well as ghost-hunting experts, authors, podcasters and presenters and their willingness to take a risk and bring paranormal investigation into the mainstream. Infinitely in debt to you all, and long may your important investigation of what is unexplained continue.

Endless love to my beautiful family and my soul dog, Arnie.

Last but by no means least, a timeless thank you to my readers and listeners all these years I have been a serial writer and podcaster. You are the stuff that dreams are made on, and the countless spooky stories and afterlife experiences you have sent me, and continue to bless me with, forever remain the spirited backbone of all my psychic world explorations.

EPITAPH

'It is wonderful that five thousand years
have now elapsed since the creation of the
world and still it is undecided whether or
not there has been an instance of the spirit
of any person appearing after death. All
argument is against it; but all belief is for it.'

Samuel Johnson

INDEX